Girlfriends

**Exploring
Women's
Relationships
in the Bible**

BARBARA J. ESSEX

The Pilgrim Press

Cleveland

To all my girlfriends
—those present and those departed—
who keep me grounded and
centered in love,
thank you for
sharing this journey.

The Pilgrim Press, 700 Prospect Avenue, Cleveland, Ohio 44115
thepilgrimpress.com
©2013 by Barbara Essex

Printed in the United States of America on acid-free paper

17   16   15   14   13   5   4   3   2   1

Library of Congress Cataloging-in-Publication Data

Essex, Barbara J. (Barbara Jean), 1951–
    Girlfriends : exploring women's relationships in the Bible /
Barbara J. Essex.
       pages cm
    ISBN 978-0-8298-1954-0 (alk. paper)
    1. Women in the Bible—Textbooks.   2. Female friendship—Biblical
teaching—Textbooks.   3. Female friendship—Religious aspects—
Christianity—Textbooks.   4. Women in mass media—Textbooks.
5. Mass media—Religious aspects—Christianity—Textbooks.   I. Title.

BS575.E885 2013
220.9′2082—dc23   2012044614

CONTENTS

GETTING STARTED

Girlfriends: Exploring Women's Relationships in the Bible is a ten-week Bible study for individuals or groups. Each Bible study explores the stories of selected biblical women and their relationships. The outline for each study unit is the same:

- **Read** focuses on a particular passage of scripture; it is recommended that you read the text before moving into the Bible study.

- **The Back Story** provides background information on the text. This section includes information to help you get into the text, information about the biblical context of the story, and anything else that will help you gain a fuller understanding of the text.

- **The Episode** focuses on a particular incident or event that involves the relationship between or among biblical women.

- **The Contemporary Connection** highlights some aspects of the biblical text that mirror contemporary situations between and among women; this section may include incidents from the author's experience of relationships with women.

- **Food for Thought** raises questions for discussion or reflection; these questions relate to the Bible study and Contemporary Connection.

- **Films and Television Shows** suggests viewing resources that illustrate aspects of the Bible study and Contemporary Connection; this section includes discussion and reflection questions about the viewing suggestions. It is not necessary to view films or shows in order to study the units. Films and television shows are readily available from your local library or video store, on your computer, or on your television (some shows are still running).

You will need at least an hour for the Bible studies—more time if you decide to watch a movie or television show. Feel free to adjust the time to suit your situation. You will need a Bible, this book, and a notebook or journal to write down your thoughts and reflections on the lessons. At the end of this book, you will find a list of resources for further study.

The Bible studies are designed so that leadership for the sessions can be rotated; you do not have to be a Bible scholar to lead the sessions. It is preferable, however, that the study units are read before the actual session. A simple format for each session can be to start the session with prayer, read the scripture, use the discussion questions to begin your conversation, and then close with prayer.

You may want to set some "ground rules" beforehand so that your session runs smoothly. There are no hard or fast rules—you want to make sure that all who want to speak may do so comfortably. Your guidelines might include these:

- Speak only for yourself; use "I" statements.
- Say only what is comfortable for you to share.
- Confidentiality is to be respected.
- Everyone's opinion is valued.

- It's okay to pass; don't feel pressured to speak.

- Respect silence.

- Do not overparticipate or underparticipate; do not monopolize the conversation.

- All questions are valid; there are no dumb questions.

- Humor is appreciated.

- Do not interrupt when someone is speaking.

- Ask questions for clarification, not to judge.

You may want to add others or come up with your own set of guidelines for conversation and comfort.

The aim of the Bible studies is to be informative and fun. Enjoy yourself!

ACKNOWLEDGEMENTS

Writers do not work in a vacuum—we are surrounded by family and friends who support, encourage, and push us to get the work done. I am grateful to all who make my life rich, warm, and stable; the usual suspects know who they are.

Thank you to the folks at The Pilgrim Press for their partnership in creating Bible studies that focus on women's issues and concerns. These resources help to fill a gap for women who hunger for informative and fun aids to bring the Bible alive for them. I am happy to contribute to the tradition of serious Bible study.

I appreciate the support and encouragement of Kim Martin Sadler, Janice Brown, Aimeé Jannsohn, and all those who bring my words to print.

As ever, any strength of this volume is due to the input and feedback from my conversation partners. For all weaknesses, I am solely responsible.

INTRODUCTION

WOMEN AND FRIENDSHIPS

BFF—in a world of "text speak," we are sometimes confused by all the letters we encounter in print and in speech. OMG, BTW, BRB, ROFL, LOL[1] . . . the new shorthand of communicating is the language of our age. I confess that I had to ask my twenty-something cousin what "BFF" stands for; when she told me, I was ROFL —"best friend forever," indeed.

My first encounter with the whole BFF thing was watching the volatile relationship between Nicole Ritchie and Paris Hilton played out on TV. The term is supposed to convey closeness between two people. Ironically, the relationship between Ritchie and Hilton seemed based on popularity, looks, and wealth. This much publicized relationship seemed so typical of celebrity life—superficial, episodic, and drama-filled. One week, they were closer than close; the next, they weren't speaking to each other. The short list of BFFs changed as often as the celebrities changed (designer) shoes. Theirs and other celebrity friendships highlighted all that we often cynically suspect of women and friendships: days filled with jealousy, backbiting, competition, and inauthenticity.

Friendship will mean different things to different people, and the Bible can help us understand the nature of our relationships better. While the Bible does not focus on friendships among women specifically, there are episodes that are instructive in the ways that women relate to each other. Friendships may change over the course of time. There may be categories of friendship—best friends, causal friends, work friends—the range is endless. The friends of our youth may not be the friends of our golden age—and, then again, they may. Friendships are important—we are learning that having friends is good for our health. Studies indicate that having good friends lowers blood pressure and strengthens the immune system.[2] In addition, friendships keep us in touch with who we are, where we have been, and where we are headed.

Life today can be hectic and it is easy to feel alone and isolated. Friendships keep us connected to others who know us and to those whom we know. There is an African proverb that states "I am because we are." And this holds true for friendships. When we are feeling blue or when we question our purpose in life, a friend can lift our spirits and remind us that we are loved. Friends help widen our world and provide opportunities to explore more deeply our hungers and needs. We need friends in order to grow; friends are more than social fillers—they rescue us from ourselves by showing that there's more to life than our current circumstances.

When I think about women and friendships, I think of my late mother. She embodied hospitality—our home was always open to receive guests. She shared special times with other women in our family, who looked to her for advice and support. They consulted her as they sought strategies for managing their marriages; and my mother was a willing mentor even as she struggled with issues in her marriage and life. Around the kitchen table, the women would share the joys and pains of being women in relationships with men. Their conversations were laced with embarrassed laughter and confessions about sexual things—they would whisper or ask me to leave the room, as if I had no clue about what they were talking about. They shared fairly openly with each other, especially the younger women, who thought my mother was wiser because of her age and because of the longevity of her marriage.

My own friendships are peppered with joy and pain. Early on, I wanted to fit in and twisted myself to do so. I worked to overcome my shyness, insecurities, and passivity to make friends. The girls I wanted most to be friends with were Brenda and Gail. They were well-dressed, smart, and popular. In my eyes, they were terrific girls who always seemed to have it all together. From them, I learned about piano lessons, dance recitals, and going to the hair salon. I loved hearing stories about their lives, which seemed so much more interesting than my own.

But Brenda and Gail seemed to go out of their way to make me feel small and "less than." They laughed at me and talked about me behind my back. They thought my questions were silly; they put me down because I wore homemade dresses. I never understood why they didn't like me. My relationships with them were marked by jealousy (on my part) and betrayal (on their parts). But I kept trying to be friends with them. That is, until one day, in the girls' restroom, I overheard them ripping me apart. They called me silly, stupid, and country. Their remarks were mean, cruel, and hurtful. No wonder I felt insecure with them. From that day on, I realized and finally accepted that they were not my friends—not my real friends.

Instead of forcing my way into their lives, I started paying more attention to the girls who wanted to spend time with me. I established new relationships with girls who enjoyed jumping rope, playing jacks, and talking about what we wanted when we grew up. With Maxine, Sharon, Loretta, and Deborah, I could laugh and play without pretensions, and we had good old-fashioned fun. I no longer had to twist myself into something I wasn't in order to fit in—I was accepted for who I was. It was a liberating feeling, although I would not have said it that way—I was accepted unconditionally and never felt the need to protect myself.

Later, as I grew more secure, I developed friendships with girls who were loyal, interesting, and interested in me and my thoughts and feelings. They were not the most popular girls and did not wear the latest fashions. In many ways, they too had been excluded for one reason or another. There was a camaraderie among us that only those on the outside understand. Some were not close friends but would come to my rescue when I needed them, and I would do the same for them. We found ways to support each other and enjoyed each other's company. Some of us lived nearby and would get together during the summer to hang out. It's safe to say that I didn't have a lot of girlfriends, but the ones I had were fabulous! We spent hours together in school and more hours on the phone or at each other's homes.

As I've grown older, I've come to rely on my friends more and more. I am part of a small yet close-knit circle of women with whom I'm able to share my secrets, hopes, dreams, and disappointments. These are the women who listen without judging and who know just the right thing to say, even when I don't want to hear it. They are women whom I trust and love. They remind me that I am not alone in the world. They make me laugh and tell me it's okay to cry. These women have been with me through thick and thin—they are my friends. Some I've known since elementary and high school and some are new to my life. We all share something in common—a concern for each other and a real interest in what is happening in each others' lives. We get together and remember the days when . . . we were young, we were skinny, we were energetic, we were foolishly in love with the wrong boys . . . filling in those blanks is so much fun as we call forth memories of our youth. We remember so much about each other, and it feels good to be with a group of women who "know" you, knew you when, and care enough to keep the friendships going.

As I stated earlier, friendships can change over time. Our circumstances change along with our interests. Those things that held us together at one phase of our lives may not be strong enough to hold us together when we start dating seriously or get married or have children. Geography may be a challenge when one friend relocates for work or marriage. Sometimes we may take a "vacation" from a friendship and discover we are connected or that it's okay to move on. Friends move in and out of our lives—sometimes the transition is easy and relatively painless; at other times the loss of a friend can cause us stress and concern.

We discover that some of these relationships are not perfect—we have our misunderstandings, times when we don't keep in touch as diligently as we'd like, missed opportunities to support one another, and overlooked birthdays, anniversaries, and milestones—yet we are held together by something that seems bigger than ourselves and the immediacy of our lives. When we don't hear from each other, we get in touch. When we argue, we find ways to make up. When we step on toes, we apologize. When we need each other, we make an effort to be there. As we age, we recognize that life is short and we relish every chance to connect and be together. My mantra of late is "We never know when the last time will be the *last* time!" This helps me to be intentional about reaching out and spurs me to make the phone call, send the e-mail, mail the card—whatever it takes to let the other know that I'm thinking about her.

I have friends with whom I am in regular contact—we talk every week, even when we don't have much to say. We giggle about events in the past, make fun of the latest celebrity news, bemoan the conditions of the world, and sigh over new hopes and dreams. We laugh at our mistakes and rant over things that make us angry. We consult each other about decisions we have to make about our health, our money, our children, our homes. We listen to each other as we go on and on about past mistakes and regrets. Even more, we challenge each other to be better people, to get over ourselves, to do something for others, to be content with our lives, and to count our blessings. We rejoice with each other and we mourn, when it is needed and appropriate. We remind each other of the good times and how we overcame challenges and obstacles. We help each other understand processes of aging—there are few subjects that are off limits. We are still learning about each other, even though we've been friends for more than forty years.

Then there are friends with whom I'm rarely in touch; we might go months or even years with no contact whatsoever. Yet when we finally talk, it's as if no time has lapsed. I count them among my closest and dearest although we don't communicate regularly or often. We don't mind the lapse in communication because we know we are just a phone call, text message, or e-mail away. There is something mystical about these friendships in that the connection remains strong without the ongoing nurture that friendships usually need. We don't feel neglected or ignored during the down times; somehow, we just know that the other is there and will be available when we need each other. There is genuine delight when we hear from each other and an eagerness to catch up with each other's lives.

Through the research, writings, and images being constructed by women, we are learning that genuine friendships are life-changing and life-giving. When women allow themselves to be in healthy relationships with other women, they find a safe place to share their thoughts and feelings without judgment. The operative word is "allow." And that is not always an easy thing to do. Through the works of sociologists and psychologists, we are learning more about what friendships between women can mean. We are learning that women want (and need) persons other than their spouses, partners, and mothers to talk to about the things that are important to them. At the same time, we are finding a growing list of resources that provide insights on how to establish, maintain, and end friendships.

We ought not to be surprised that so much has been made of men's relationships. From the days of Aristotle, much has been written historically about men's relationships with other men. In fact, men's friendships were considered the highest expression of relationships, valued even over marital ones. Women were seen as inferior and relationships with them were tainted by romantic and sexual feelings. Platonic relationships among men were lifted up.

While much of the historical literature about friendship focused on men, women's relationships were not considered worthy of notice. Women were discouraged from writing and publishing their thoughts and feelings. As we scan literature from ages past, we are struck by the lack of substantial writings about women and friendships. Fortunately, that trend is turning around with a wide range of materials and research now dealing with women and friendships—written by women and for women. Today, we are now seeing more written about women and their relationships with other women.

In modern times, men's relationships shifted from those of respect, honor, and integrity among peers to those marked by competition and a reluctance to show weakness or vulnerability. In the twentieth and twenty-first century, we are seeing a movement among men who seek more authentic relationships with men. Generally speaking, it has been noted that men connect around common interests and skills while women connect around shared feelings—women are more likely to join informal and formal groups to help them deal with particular concerns.

What are some characteristics of healthy friendships? In their collaborative work *I Know Just What You Mean*, authors Ellen Goodman and Gail O'Brien make these observations[3]:

- Having and being a friend means you know and accept the other and you are, in turn, known and accepted.
- Each makes the time and effort to understand the other, deeply and unconditionally.
- Trust is the foundation for the friendship, allowing each to share her worries and secrets.

- Loyalty is required, knowing that you can count on the other to be on your side.
- Friendship means knowing that you can depend on the other and that she can depend on you; your friend shows up when it counts.

Basic characteristics of friendship include good listening skills, the capacity to empathize, and a willingness to be there. In stressful and dangerous situations, men move towards flight or fight while women move towards "tend and befriend," that is, taking care of the children and gathering with other women.[4]

Despite the evidence that highlights the benefits of friendships, some women have a difficult time connecting with other women. There are many reasons for women avoiding friendships with other women—who needs all the problems? Sometimes it is difficult to establish meaningful friendships because of jealousy, competition for men's attention and affection, insecurities, or past experiences of betrayal and mistrust. Some women deny that they need relationships beyond their families. How many women have you met who say that their husbands are their best friends? And for some, this is true and right for them. Others want something else—not better, just something else. There are things that only other women can understand.

In our mobile culture, people may not stay in one place long enough to develop deep connections. The emergence of online "social networks" seeks to connect people with each other. We are hard pressed to find anyone who has not at least heard of Facebook, Twitter, and MySpace. Many folks have e-mail accounts and use the technology to keep their friends and acquaintances informed about their lives. People work at keeping in touch with each other—by phone, mail, e-mail, text, Skype—you name it. These methods work for many people; others prefer the "good old-fashioned" method of face-to-face conversation.

This group of Bible studies is designed to get us thinking about those friendships that hold us together. There is a mystery about friendships—we are not always clear about how we establish friendships or how we maintain and nurture them. In many ways, these friendships just *are*. They are gifts that carry those things that make us feel good about who we are and our place in the world. They keep us centered, balanced, and grounded. Our friends comfort and support us; they challenge and critique us—always in the name of love.

WOMEN AND THE BIBLE

Women's relationships are not prominent in the Bible. In many cases, women appear in order to advance the story of males—they either support or hinder the advancement of men. Women play various roles in the Bible, but we are not often privy to their thoughts, feelings, hopes, and dreams—although there are, of course, exceptions. We are able to eavesdrop on Hannah, Esther, Ruth, Naomi, and Mary the mother of Jesus to learn something of their thoughts, feelings, hopes, and fears. While their stories are parts of larger narratives, they stand out and we learn much about them.

In recent years, more biblical scholars are lifting up women. The cloak of patriarchy, though, makes unearthing women's stories quite the challenge. Patriarchy, the system of male dominance over women and children, is the framework within which the Bible was written. During biblical times, men held power in all aspects of life and society. In other words, it was all about the men. The family was the basic unit of society and family lines were traced through the father. Women's roles were limited primarily to wife and mother, though we find greater freedom for women at some times and places throughout the Bible. Women were punished more harshly for sexual offenses than were men. In most cases, women were expected to sacrifice all for family, even their very lives. Regarding women in the Bible, we are always dealing with the question of what patriarchic purpose the woman served? The answers are too often problematic and distressing.

Now, this is not to say that women had no power, for they did. And women exercised power in creative and subversive ways. Women in the Bible devised responses to patriarchy that make us laugh *and* cry. Even more challenging is trying to determine how women interacted with each other in the Bible. Despite finding a range of roles that women play in the Bible, we are not often privy to their thoughts and feelings. To make matters worse, many interactions between women in the Bible were problematic—filled with violence, betrayal, competition, judgment, jealousy, and insecurity. There are few instances of women cooperating and collaborating in the Bible. When we encounter them, we are amazed at the power women exerted and the blow they struck against patriarchy and oppression.

One way women exercised power in the Bible was as trickster. A trickster was one who changed the course of action and outcome in a text. For instance, Shiphrah and Puah, the midwives in Exodus 1, were tricksters—their refusal to kill male babies when they were born changed the course of the story and allowed Moses, the future deliverer of the Hebrew people, to avoid the genocide of the Egyptian pharaoh.

When we read the Bible, we must consider how we let the women speak for themselves, in their cultural context, without imposing our contemporary understandings on them. It is easy to say what biblical women should and ought to do—but their reality was different from ours. And even our own cultural understandings are not unified. Rather, we live within a range of understandings and freedoms, just as our ancient sisters in the Bible did. Our task as we study these women will be to let the women and their situations stand and determine what in their stories resonates with our contemporary situations and circumstances.

WOMEN, THE BIBLE, AND POPULAR CULTURE

There is a renewed interest in exploring women's lives in nonfiction and fiction, in film and on television. We owe much of this interest to the feminist movement(s) having lifted up the importance of women and their stories. The feminist perspective is that women matter and should enjoy the privileges that men enjoy but have been denied because of gender. Feminism shines a spotlight on things that matter to women and that make life better for women and men.

While there are barriers to friendships, there are more reasons for women to connect. The issues of race, class, nationality, religion, ability, and sexual orientation are real and can be building blocks for women working together in new and creative ways. Films like *9 to 5* show what women can achieve by collaborating to deal with sexism, racism, and other "isms" in the workplace. We spend a great deal of time at work, and it is important to have a safe environment where all are able to do their best work. Women can find ways to cooperate and collaborate around issues that concern them. But workplace collaboration is not necessarily friendship.

Friendship is more than working in utilitarian ways for a greater good. Friendships allow us to connect with one another, to share parts of ourselves, and to know that we will not be exploited or abused. Friendships become safe harbors within which we can explore who we are and what our purposes for living are. In addition, friendships remind us that we are not alone in the world, that there are those who love us and whom we love. We are part of a web of relationships and connections that give meaning to our lives. We become part of an extended family where we can ask for what we need and give in return.

Some even suggest that the need to connect is part of the human condition. We women are at our best when we are in friendships with other women that are marked by love, trust, support, and affirmation. A good friend does more than gossip with us—she encourages and challenges us and lets us know that she is on our side.

Women's literature, film, and music help us explore our relationships and broaden our worldview. Sometimes labeled as "chick flicks" and "chick lit," these venues can serve the higher purpose of helping us all—women and men—understand who we are individually and who we are as part of a social network. Chick flicks and literature about women are said to be sappy and saccharine because their mostly female characters engage in extended dialogue and tap into the characters' emotions. The plot lines tend to be predictable and focused on romance, money, and relationships. But increasingly films depict women in real life situations and offer some interesting ways of looking at them. For instance, *Real Women Have Curves* (2002) is a film about a Mexican American young woman who is seeking a sense of herself apart from her family and its traditions, and *Notes on a Scandal* (2006) deals with friendship and mental instability.

The Bible, though an ancient book, is also relevant for us today. The situations and circumstances in the Bible still occur today. As the preacher in Ecclesiastes (Eccl. 1:9) says,

What has been is what will be,
and what has been done is what will be done;
there is nothing new under the sun.

I am always on the hunt for resources that help us understand the human condition and connect to the biblical texts. Chick flicks and lit provide ample examples to illustrate the essence of the biblical text, and the Bible does the same for real life. Both popular culture and biblical study help us delve into matters that we encounter in life. For each chapter of this book, I suggest films and television shows that connect with the biblical story. While the Bible does not specifically focus on women's relationships, there are a number of situations where women are working together or working against each other. My question is always, "What can we learn from this story?"

No doubt, you will wonder why I have chosen a particular film or show; some will support the biblical lesson and some will not. The films and shows are chosen because they touch on the Bible in some way. You may have suggestions that fit better. Please feel free to choose your own—make it fun and interesting.

Under "The Contemporary Connection," I tie together the biblical text and contemporary life as it is expressed in popular culture, such as in films and television shows. These venues reflect values and perspectives in their time periods and help us understand better who we are and what motivates us. Some make us take a long hard look at ourselves and help us examine what we want out of life. Most are short on action, but they serve a purpose. They provide fodder for real-life conversations and explorations. Good film and literature help us explore our lives and challenge us to be clearer about what we believe and value.

I am drawn to films that make me feel and think. I prefer complex and layered movies that take me to places in my head and heart that are different from my reality. Old movies, especially black and white ones, are among my favorites. There were a number of female-focused films from 1930 to 1950 with big name stars: Barbara Stanwyck, Bette Davis, Joan Crawford, Lana Turner, Marilyn Monroe, Carole Lombard, Jean Harlow, Greta Garbo, Lauren Bacall, Rita Hayworth, Audrey Hepburn, Katherine Hepburn—the list is not diverse racially and ethnically, a sign of the times. However, these women and others played a range of characters—independent, career-minded, strong, beautiful, insecure, mentally disturbed—some women who took care of themselves and others who were dependent for various reasons. In these old movies, the women were long-suffering and went to great lengths to survive and triumph over their various trials and tribulations. Directors used lighting, music, and dialogue to move the story forward. The films dealt with a number of issues: to marry or not; to have children or not; workplace concerns; war; love and romance; family dynamics; aging; and criminality.

Contemporary Hollywood films tend to be more commercial with fairly predictable plots. Casting choices are curious yet actresses are able to breathe life into a script and make the film come alive for us. Contemporary artists include Meryl Streep, CCH Pounder, Hattie McDaniel, Dorothy Dandridge, Eartha Kitt, Halle Berry, Julia Roberts, Jessica Alba, Salma Hayek, Lauren Velez, Lucy Liu, Sandra Oh, America Ferrera, Helen Mirren, Angela Bassett, Jennifer Aniston, Meg Ryan, Ruby Dee, Goldie Hawn, Bette Midler, Diane Keaton, Nicole Kidman, Judi Dench, Margaret Cho, Whoopi Goldberg, Glenn Close, Diahann Carroll, Angelina Jolie, and Cate Blanchett. These women and others have played a range of roles, from drug addicts and unfit mothers to doctors, lawyers, and international spies. They continue the legacy of lifting up women's concerns and perspectives. In addition, women are playing action hero roles—they fight, shoot, engage in high-speed chases, and blow up buildings and bridges—just like men! I'm not saying this is a good thing necessarily, but women are not limited to "traditional" roles of wife and mother. They are expanding our conception of what women can do and be.

Serial television shows offer a longer timeline in which to observe characters. There are not a lot of television shows that focus on women and women's concerns. The exceptions stand out for us: *I Love Lucy, The Mary Tyler Moore Show, Cagney and Lacey, Designing Women, The Golden Girls, Girlfriends, Living Single,* and *Desperate Housewives* are among them. These shows provide entertainment and help us laugh at our own foibles when we start to take ourselves too seriously.

While not a big fan of "reality shows," I believe some show us slices of life that make us take a look out at ourselves; they force us to judge and that can be helpful in determining why we are drawn to or repulsed by certain behaviors and situations. Many reality shows are over the top and the drama seems forced. Shows like *Next Top Model* and *The Real Housewives of* _____ (you name the city) make us wonder how much is real and how much is staged. But if we look at them as glimpses into lives, we may be able to glean some learnings from them. Of course, these shows stress competition, backbiting, insincerity—all the stereotypes of women we are trying to overcome.

In works of fiction, we find a range of female relationships. Some authors—Toni Morrison, J. K. Rowling, Margaret Atwood, Alice Walker, Gloria Naylor, Amy Tan, Sandra Cisneros, Isabel Allende, Jane Austen, Louisa May Alcott, Doris Lessing, and Willa Cather among others—give us believable characters who teach us as they learn. Coming-of-age works resonant with us because we see ourselves in them—most of us have had awkward moments from our childhoods that we want to forget. Good literature helps us face those moments and learn something that helps us be stronger and wiser. The literature helps us figure out our own dilemmas and explore possibilities.

I have tried to identify films and television shows that are readily available, either because the show is currently on television or because the films and shows are available on DVD or the Internet. Some are older resources and some are fairly recent. All deal with some aspect of women and friendships and run the gamut from healthy to unhealthy connections.

My hope is that you will watch some films and shows as a group and use them as the basis for your conversation about the texts and stories from the Bible. Bible study can be fun, and to couple it with contemporary resources can enhance and enrich the Bible—and help us see ourselves in the biblical story. Here's hoping for a wonderful adventure as you explore the ties that bind.

Food for Thought

1. What is your definition of "friendship"? When did you first realize you had a "friend"?

2. What do you expect from a friend? What kind of friend are you?

3. What obstacles have you encountered in making friends? What have been your experiences of rejecting the overtures for friendships?

4. What are a few of your favorite movies and/or television shows? What is appealing to you about them? Have you ever considered them alongside the Bible? Why or why not?

5. Why do you think women's relationships are so negative in the Bible?

1

SARAH AND HAGAR

Okay, I know what you're thinking . . . Sarah and Hagar friends? By no stretch of the imagination can we even think that these two are friends. They are locked in a triangle of power, sex, and baby mama drama. Let's see what we can learn from these two strong women and their situation.

Read

Genesis 16:1–16 and Genesis 21:1–21

The Back Story

Encounters between Sarah and Hagar take place within the larger story of Abraham. There are a lot of women in the Bible who are mothers—some are named and others are not. Almost all of them are tied to men in their lives: fathers, brothers, husbands, uncles, and rulers. The basic unit of biblical culture is the family headed by a male who has responsibility for the entire household. The expectation for women is that they remain in their father's home until they marry. Then the women are to have children, preferably males, because the bloodline is traced through the father. The wife's role includes living honorably so as not to bring shame upon her husband, caring for and educating the children, and making sure the private sphere of the household runs smoothly.

The role of mother is taken seriously in biblical culture. Women who are not able to produce children are of particular interest in the Bible. Fertility is a sign of blessing, which makes infertility a major problem.[1] Women are blamed for childlessness; it's never the man's "fault." Fertility points to God, who opens up and closes wombs of women for a number of reasons. The inability to have children is seen as a curse, and extraordinary measures are taken to ensure that men have male heirs to carry on the family.

One measure to ensure children is the levirate marriage. If a woman's husband dies without (male) heirs, his brother is allowed (indeed, urged) to marry the widow. The firstborn son of this union legally belongs to the dead husband, not the living brother. If a brother does not carry out the levirate marriage, he brings shame to the entire family.

Another measure is for the wife to provide a suitable substitute to serve as a surrogate; the substitute is usually a servant or slave. The child produced by the husband and surrogate legally belongs to the wife, not the birth mother. In this episode, Sarah and Hagar are caught in a triangle that advances promises God made to Abraham.

God promises to make Abraham the father of a great nation with a population so numerous that they outnumber the grains of sand on the beach (see Gen. 12:1–3). This grandiose promise wouldn't be so bad except that Abraham's wife, Sarah, is unable to have children (see Gen. 11:30, 16:1). And, as we know, humans sometimes feel the need to help God out, and that's what Sarah does. She offers her servant, Hagar, to be a surrogate mother.

The Egyptian Hagar is Sarah's maid servant, perhaps as part of Pharaoh's gifts to Abraham during his sojourn in Egypt (see Gen. 12:10ff). It may be that Hagar was one of Sarah's servants while she lived in Pharaoh's palace and Sarah was allowed to keep her as a kind of parting gift. While we don't know the specifics of how Hagar came to live with Abraham and Sarah, we know that she occupies an inferior position to Sarah—she is a single woman, a foreign woman, and a servant woman. Hagar belongs to Sarah and is under her complete control and power. Hagar has no choice but to have sex with Abraham. We don't know how she feels about this or if she protests.

However, we know that Abraham does not protest. The practice was a way to make sure he had heirs. The child born to Hagar legally belongs to Sarah since Hagar legally belongs to Sarah. Hagar has no rights that would be respected by Hebrew law.

The Episode

Sarah gives Hagar to Abraham to be his wife (see Gen. 16:3b) as if she were Hagar's father. Remember that this is not a romantic liaison; Abraham is only having sexual relations with Hagar to conceive a child that will help fulfill God's promise of progeny for Abraham. Hagar conceives and things should run smoothly because Abraham is now well on the way to becoming a father. Abraham is happy; God is happy; but Sarah and Hagar have a rough time of it.

Early on, Sarah holds the power because she determines the fate of Hagar, who is a servant (slave). When Hagar gets pregnant, however, her attitude changes from obedience (we assume) to one of contempt. Hagar knows she has the upper hand because she is carrying Abraham's child. Hagar now holds the power. Although her child legally belongs to Sarah, Hagar knows that she is doing something that Sarah cannot—give birth to Abraham's child.

Even though Sarah knows that the child will legally belong to her, she cannot bear insubordinate behavior from her servant.

Sarah speaks to Abraham about it, but Abraham continues the track that she has started—he didn't initiate the relationship between himself and Hagar and cannot now intervene. Abraham makes Sarah the power broker in this situation. Sarah does not try to work things out with Hagar; she sees violence as her only choice and deals harshly with Hagar. Her treatment is too much for Hagar.

Hagar knows that appealing to Abraham will be no use. Hagar, pushed to the limit, sees fleeing as her only option. Although pregnant, and having no rights or resources, she leaves Abraham's household to take her chances in the wilderness.

Because the story is about Abraham and not really about the women, we don't have information about what actually happened between Sarah and Hagar. Both women resort to extreme individual behaviors rather than collaborate with each other. Sarah feels disrespected and Hagar feels abused. Both are right. The fact that Abraham does not step in means that both women are left to their own devices as they cope with the situation. Both women do what they feel they have to do; the consequences don't bode well for anyone in the Abraham household. Abraham has to endure the shame of not protecting the child to be born, and he also runs the risk of not having any children to ensure the future of his family. For Sarah, any chance of providing a child for Abraham is dashed, unless she provides another surrogate. And Hagar learns the hard way that she cannot count on being protected or having a safe place to deliver her child. This is a fiasco that makes the home rife with tension and stress and danger.

Hagar decides to leave the household. In some ways, this is positive because she understands her limits and knows that she does have options. That her options don't seem practical is beside the point; the dangers of the wilderness seem preferable to the abuse she suffers at Sarah's hands. We assume that she heads towards Egypt, her home. Her life and that of her unborn child is in jeopardy as she sojourns in the wilderness—she has no means to protect herself and it is not clear if she will survive. She is at the mercy of the elements, wild animals, and robbers who prey on travelers. Her trek is dangerous because there are few resources to help her and certainly few places to offer hospitality and rest. About halfway home, she stops by a spring of water in Shur, near the northeast border of Egypt. She has an encounter with an angel of God, who orders her to return to Sarah and Abraham. She does—and we might question why she is ordered to return to a place of violence and abuse.

What we can speculate is that her survival depends on her being in community. In ancient and contemporary times, childbirth carried risks for the mother and the child. Hagar cannot deliver her baby alone and certainly not in the wilderness. God promises her that her future will be bright—her son will take care of her. Hagar also receives a promise from God that parallels Abraham's. She will have a multitude of offspring. Hagar is the only woman in the Bible to name God, signifying the significance of her encounter with the God who finds her and rescues her (see Gen. 16:7–14). Despite being a woman and a foreigner, Hagar is empowered and affirmed by the God who finds her in the wilderness and rescues her from certain death. Her encounter with God is powerful, and God does not leave her alone to perish.

Hagar goes back and delivers a healthy son, who is named Ishmael. Back at Abraham's, she has shelter, food, and other women to help deliver her baby. We can assume that the situation between herself and Sarah continues to be strained. She is part of a blended family. The text is silent about the atmosphere of the Abraham household but we can imagine how difficult the situation is.

We soon learn that Sarah becomes pregnant despite all the odds against her (see Gen. 17:15–16; 21:1–7). God is gracious and blesses her with a son. And we learn that the blended family situation really doesn't work for Sarah. With her own son now, she has no need for Hagar and Ishmael. She insists that Abraham banish the woman and her son from the home. Abraham reacts with misgivings and seeks some way to keep both boys at home (see Gen. 17:18–21). Abraham's concern is for the firstborn son, who stands to inherit the major portion of Abraham's legacy. However, God seems to favor the second child, Isaac, and encourages Abraham to listen to Sarah and to send Hagar and Ishmael away (see Gen. 21:8–14).

For the second time, Hagar leaves Abraham's home—the first time, she decided to leave; this time, she is forced to leave because of Sarah's jealousy and insecurity. Yet in her exile both times, Hagar discovers a God who sees, hears, and rescues. Sarah is a major actor in both episodes—the first time, she abuses Hagar so much that the servant sees no option but to leave; this time, she voices her disdain and commands Abraham to get rid of Hagar and her son.

Clearly, we cannot say that Sarah and Hagar are friends. They are at odds with each other and the household is, no doubt, filled with tension and animosity. The two women are never shown interacting with each other—they never speak to each other. Sarah speaks to Abraham and Hagar speaks to God. They cannot resolve their differences if they are not able (or willing) to talk to each other. Sarah feels threatened and Hagar feels exploited—at least, that is a reasonable conclusion we can draw. Because we have no indication of their feelings, we can only guess at what is happening within them as they try to deal with a situation that seems out of their control.

The Contemporary Connection

The situation between Sarah and Hagar is played out in popular culture with some variations. Sarah, wanting a child to help fulfill

God's promise to her husband, takes matters in her own hands. She gives her husband permission to sleep with her servant. Hagar is not consulted and she becomes a pawn in the Abraham household. Hagar is an object and her status as slave means she has no recourse except to do as she is told.

Hagar understands that her status changes once she becomes pregnant. Her demeanor changes to the point of insubordination. When Sarah begins to abuse her, Hagar can only take so much. She makes the decision to leave the household, and Abraham does nothing to stop her. She would rather risk death in the wilderness than stay and put up with the abuse that Sarah dishes out upon her.

Today, we might say that both Sarah and Hagar missed an opportunity to model what a healthy blended family could be. Both women are strong in their own ways. Sarah is a communicator and makes her husband listen to her. She exercises power in her marital relationship. She understands "attitude" when it is directed to her and she knows her limits. Her self-esteem is healthy enough to know when she's had enough but not strong enough to find a way to make things work.

Hagar, though a slave, knows her worth. When she becomes pregnant, she changes—perhaps not for the better. But she, too, knows when she's had enough. When the situation with Sarah becomes unbearable, Hagar has the courage to leave. Now, we might assume that her flight is ill-planned since she doesn't have enough of what she needs to make the long trek home. She feels she can make it on her own. But when ordered back, she is courageous enough to go back into a bad situation for the sake of her child. We don't know the indignities she might have suffered upon her return. But she delivers a healthy baby. Despite having been banished from Abraham's home, she manages to raise her son. She finds a suitable wife for him and he takes care of her until she dies. If nothing else, Hagar knows how to survive.

Together, Sarah and Hagar would have been a formidable force. They could have worked together to raise strong, centered, and grounded children. They could have shared each other's culture and wisdom for the sake of the children. These two mothers could have embodied the African proverb "it takes a village to raise a child." Sarah's mature wisdom would have balanced Hagar's impulsive, youthful idealism. By focusing their energies on the children, they could have cooperated and collaborated in wonderful ways.

We don't see either woman engaged with other women. They don't seem to have a circle of friends to advise or listen to them. They are dependent on Abraham as their sole shoulder on which to lean. We don't even see him interacting with Hagar—she is truly a woman alone. We wonder if a circle of caring girlfriends would have made a difference for either woman.

There are real-life models of women working together for the sake of their children. A well-documented case is that of Jada Pinkett Smith and Sheree Zampinio. Jada is the current wife of actor and entertainer Will Smith, who had a son, Trey, with first wife Sheree. Will and Jada appeared on an episode of the Oprah Show to discuss their lives (for a video clip, see "Mr. and Mrs. Smith," http://www.oprah.com/oprahshow/Will-Smith-and-Jada-Pinkett-Smith-Talk-Family). They highlighted the collaboration between Jada and Sheree, who found ways to put aside whatever personal feelings they had in order to make all the children feel loved and safe. Jada, a child of divorced parents, did not want Trey to feel abandoned or left out. These days, Sheree and her husband attend Smith family gatherings—all the children see their parents and stepparents getting along, and this example helps them to know that people can create harmonious relationships. Jada confessed that she had some difficulties at first but soon realized that it wasn't about her—it was about the children, putting them first, and creating a family in which they could all thrive. Sarah and Hagar could have learned a lesson from Jada and Sheree.

Food for Thought

1. How do you make friends with other women? What barriers have you crossed to establish and nurture friendships with other women? What are the benefits and risks of reaching out to other women?

2. Sarah and Hagar are in conflict with each other with Abraham at the center. This situation makes friendship between the two women challenging. In what ways have you experienced conflict with another woman over the attention or affection of another person?

3. How can women overcome issues with each other to form coalitions to help each other? How can women learn to trust each other?

4. Name the images of mothers and stepmothers who are portrayed in popular culture. In what ways are the portrayals accurate? In what ways are they unrealistic? Who is served by the various images—that is, who profits or gains from the ways women are portrayed?

5. Celebrity couple and actors Will Smith and wife Jada Pinkett Smith have found a way to make their blended family work by putting the children first. What keeps women at odds with each other in cases of divorce and remarriage? How can women overcome jealousy and competition in order to raise healthy, happy children?

Films and Television Shows

Stepmom (1998), starring Susan Sarandon and Julia Roberts, is a film about women learning to work together after a rocky beginning. Jackie (Susan Sarandon) is the divorced mother of two children. Her ex-husband Luke (Ed Harris) is involved with a younger woman, Isabel (Julia Roberts). Jackie lives with her children in the country far from the hustle and bustle of her previous

Manhattan life as an editor. Luke, an attorney who still lives in the city, has the children on the weekends. More and more, he abdicates the care of the children to his girlfriend Isabel, a fashion photographer, who is not experienced with caring for children. When Jackie learns that she has cancer, she realizes that she needs someone to take care of her children. This begins a journey for these two women, who must figure out how to co-exist. It is a heartwarming story of jealousy, competition, and, finally, cooperation and respect.

As you watch the film, pay attention to the relationships Jackie has with her children, especially her daughter.

- Are there parallels between the biblical story and the film? What are they? Who symbolizes Sarah in the film? Who symbolizes Hagar? Is there an Abraham figure in the film?

- How does Jackie's relationships with her children change over the course of the film?

- How does Isabel try to make the relationship with her stepchildren work? What role does Luke play in the way the story unfolds?

- What is the turning point in the film? How does the turning point influence and reshape the relationship between Jackie and Isabel? Jackie and her children? Isabel and her stepchildren?

- How do you think the future unfolds for this family?

The First Wives' Club (1996), based on a novel by Olivia Goldsmith, is the story of three friends who are reunited after twenty-seven years at the funeral of a mutual friend. Their ex-husbands are all involved with younger women. On the surface, this film seems only to focus on revenge against men. However, there is more to the film—the women overcome their own issues with each other and with themselves to find creative ways to move on with their lives. In this case, the first wives—Brenda (Bette Midler), Elise (Goldie Hawn) and Annie (Diane Keaton)—don't just get mad, they get even.

- How do you characterize the friendship among the three first wives? What is the foundation for their friendship? Why do you think they have not kept in touch over the years?

- What lessons could the wives teach Sarah and Hagar about life and friendships?

- Why do the women in the film decide to reunite? How do they deal with each other's foibles?

- In what ways do they strengthen and encourage each other? Do you think they will stay connected as the future unfolds? Why or why not?

Passion Fish (1992) is a film that centers on the relationship between two women, May-Alice (Mary McDonnell) and Chantelle (Alfre Woodard). May-Alice plays a soap opera star who is injured in a car accident. She is forced to return to her family home in Louisiana, where she drinks heavily and abuses her caregivers. Her latest caregiver is Chantelle, who brings her own issues to her work. The animosity they have for each other eventually moves towards a friendship that is mutually beneficial. The moral of the film is that second chances are possible.

- How do you explain May-Alice's angst and depression? What is missing in her life?

- What issues does Chantelle bring to her work with May-Alice? What is missing in her life?

- What is the turning point in the film? How does this influence and reshape May-Alice and Chantelle's relationship?

- What barriers do the women have to overcome so a genuine relationship can develop? How are their challenges similar to and/or different from those of Sarah and Hagar?

- Do you think May-Alice and Chantelle will stay connected? Why or why not?

The Women (2008) is a remake of the 1939 film and is based on Clare Boothe Luce's theatrical production. The original film starred Norma Shearer (Mary), Paulette Goddard (Miriam), Rosalind Russell (Sylvia), and Joan Crawford (Crystal) and boasted an all-female cast, a rare gem in the 1930s. Divorce was difficult for women in that era and much of the comedy depended on the antics of the women to make choices for themselves.

The Hollywood remake centers on the life of the rich and naïve Mary (Meg Ryan) as she learns that her husband is having an affair with a department store sales clerk. She is at the mercy of her friends and her mom as they do their best to help her move on with her life. Her friends are Sylvie (Annette Bening), Alex (Jada Pinkett Smith), and Edie (Debra Messing). Candice Bergen plays her mom and Eva Mendes plays the other woman. Mary learns that her friends are themselves in less than satisfying romantic relationships.

As you watch the film, consider the following questions.

- How do the women become friends? What do they offer each other?

- Some of the drama in the film centers on the relationship between Mary and Sylvie. In what ways do they affirm each other? In what ways do they challenge each other?

- What does Mary learn about herself that will influence her future choices?

- What are the differences among the friends? How do they deal with their differences?

- What lessons could Mary teach Sarah about relating to women? What could she teach Hagar?

- What aspects of the film seem outdated? Which seem unrealistic?

- Are you pleased with the way the film ends? Why or why not?

2

L E A H   A N D   R A C H E L

Two sisters are at odds with each other for the love of Jacob. The competition escalates until they find common ground and work together to keep their families safe.

Read

Genesis 31:1–18

The Back Story

The stories of Rachel and Leah are part of the larger narrative about Jacob. The younger son of Isaac and Rebekah and grandson of Abraham and Sarah, Jacob is a scoundrel who cheats his older brother out of his birthright. According to custom, the elder son receives the major portion of the father's estate, but Jacob gets Esau to give up his birthright for a bowl of stew (see Gen. 25:29–34). To compound the deceit, Jacob also tricks Isaac into giving him the blessing the father gives to the elder son (see Gen. 27:30–38).

Jacob's older brother Esau is furious and plots to kill Jacob. Their mother discovers the plot and encourages Jacob to go away to Haran to stay with her brother until things cool down. When he arrives in Haran, Jacob encounters Rachel, his cousin and Laban's younger daughter. Jacob assists her and it is love at first sight (see Gen. 29:9–14). Jacob is warmly welcomed into the home of his uncle and his cousins.

Laban also has an older daughter, Leah. Of the two, Jacob wants to marry Rachel and agrees to work for Laban for seven years to earn the right to marry her. At the end of his term, which flies by, Jacob is thrown a magnificent wedding feast. Because the bride is veiled, Jacob doesn't know until the next morning that he's been duped. The bride is not Rachel, but rather her older sister, Leah, who is less desirable than Rachel (see Gen. 29:21–30). According to custom, the older daughter must marry before the younger one does. Laban asks Jacob to stay married to Leah and if he is willing to work another seven years, Jacob can marry Rachel. And Jacob agrees.

Jacob arrived in Haran a single man and wound up with two wives. He tolerates Leah and loves Rachel—the biblical text makes it clear where Jacob's heart is. But God has more in store for Jacob, whose past choices were marked by his deceiving his brother; now the tables are turned. As fate would have it, Leah is the fertile one while Rachel is barren (see Gen. 29:31). Leah starts having sons for Jacob right away. Rachel, unable to have children, envies her sister and has a nasty confrontation with Jacob (see Gen. 30:1–2). Taking matters into her own hands, Rachel provides a surrogate through her maid, Bilhah. It's like déjà vu all over again—remember Sarah and Hagar? Bilhah has two sons for Jacob. Leah still doesn't give up. When she is unable to have more children, she offers her maid, Zilpah, to Jacob. She also has sons for him.

Then, to complicate the already complex family situation, Rachel miraculously gives birth to two sons. Together, the four women give birth to twelve sons and one daughter for Jacob. Throughout the years and the drama, Jacob doesn't say much. Instead, we find chatty and active women—they give birth, name the children, compete with each other, and, among themselves, decide who will share Jacob's bed on any given night. Jacob is told by God to leave Haran and return to the land of his father. Jacob sets out towards home with his family and worldly goods.

The Episode

In the whirlwind of sibling rivalry and childbirth, the sisters, Jacob's wives, are not happy with the situation. The maids, of course, have no say in the matter. During this time, Jacob and Laban play games that center on wealth and power until God tells Jacob to return home. In an unusual move in the Bible, Jacob consults his wives about the matter and calls a family meeting with Leah and Rachel. He explains the situation to them—about how he's been tricked and deceived by his uncle. It has been Jacob's ingenuity and creativity and God's grace that enabled him to recoup his wealth. Jacob feels justified in his actions against Laban. Despite his efforts to thwart him, Laban has not succeeded in getting the best of Jacob. Jacob's righteous indignation moves the sisters to claim their allegiance to him. They feel that their father has wronged them as well. They express anger against their father and align themselves with their husband. They agree to leave Haran with Jacob.

It is not clear why Leah had not already married by the time Jacob came along. Perhaps her father had not yet found a suitable husband for her. Some suggest that she was not attractive; but in biblical culture the way one looked did not necessarily have anything to do with whether one married. What works, or should work, in her favor once she is married is the fact that she can have children. Still, winning Jacob's heart is a losing battle for Leah—clearly, Jacob does not love her. She may not be as beautiful as

Rachel and that feeds her insecurities. That Jacob desires and loves Rachel must have left a bitter taste in Leah's mouth. She has six sons and one daughter for Jacob: Reuben, Simeon, Levi, Judah, Issachar, Zebulun, and Dinah. Her servant, Zilpah, has two sons for Jacob: Gad and Asher. The text does not tell us about Leah's relationship with her daughter, the only child of hers that Leah does not name. Thinking that having children for him will make Jacob change his mind and heart towards her, she never gives up and does what she can to make Jacob love her.

Rachel understands that she is the preferred woman in the triangle of Jacob, Leah, and herself, even though she is the second wife. The text states that Jacob loves her, one of few instances in the Bible where romantic love is highlighted. She is comfortable enough to express to Jacob her anguish about her barrenness. They speak honestly to each other despite the difficulty of the situation. Jacob doesn't have any answers for her. Fertility was seen as the work of God and if there are not children born to a marriage, the woman is "blamed." There was nothing Jacob could do, except continue loving Rachel.

Rachel, in the footsteps of Sarah, gives her maid, Bilhah, to Jacob as a wife. Bilhah has two sons for him: Dan and Naphtali. Then Rachel becomes pregnant—wonder of wonders! She gives birth to Joseph, who becomes Jacob's favorite child. When Jacob decides to relocate his family to Canaan, Rachel gives birth to Benjamin, and then she dies.

Despite their differences, the sisters cooperate when Jacob prepares to leave Haran. They see their father as their common "enemy." Not only has he cheated Jacob, but also he has cheated the daughters out of their inheritance. Jacob and his wives make the choice to leave Laban. As they are preparing to leave, Rachel steals her father's household gods that symbolize his place as head of the household. And away they go—without so much as a goodbye.

When Laban hears about their departure, he and his entourage chase after them. Laban confronts Jacob, stating that Jacob cheated him out of the chance to have a going away party for his son-in-law and two daughters. Jacob states that he fled out of fear of what Laban might do to him and his family. When Laban asks why Jacob took his household gods, Jacob condemns anyone who would take the items. Laban snoops around for them—in the tents of Jacob, Leah, Bilhah, and Zilpah. When he enters Rachel's tent, she allows him to search but declares that she cannot rise from the camel's saddle to help him because she is on her period. In reality, she has hidden the gods in the saddle. Laban accepts her excuse. Jacob has his own list of grievances against Laban and states his case. Laban saves face and avoids shame by taking the high road. He and Jacob part in peace (see Gen. 31:43–50).

Both Leah and Rachel are portrayed as strong, active women. They make choices and, when they are pushed, find common ground. They are willing to give up familiar surroundings and support systems to be with Jacob. The male presence changes the family dynamics and the sibling relationship. The sisters who have been in fierce competition with each other now collaborate for the sake of the family.

The Contemporary Connection

Leah and Rachel do not break from the cultural goal of marrying and having children. We are not sure how they got along before Jacob's arrival. Certainly, after he appears on the scene, the sisters duke it out for his affection. In this situation, romantic love trumps familial ties.

There are many examples of women in triangular relationships with men. In most cases, the wife and the "other" woman are at odds with each other while the husband gets the best of the married and single life. The women are left to deal with each other, and rarely do they deal with the man. At least, this is the picture most often portrayed in films and is generally accepted as the way things are. We have heard over and over again the adage that "boys will be boys." This seems true even when public figures and leaders are in the spotlight. The infidelity of former President William Clinton is only one example of how men are excused for their behavior.

In many triangular situations, everyone loses and the lines of accountability are not clear. In too many cases, the men are allowed to move on without much difficulty. The women, however, become collateral damage and may find themselves in dire straits. When children are part of the relationships, they can become pawns in the adult relationships and this can be quite messy.

There is a cultural expectation that sisters will support and love each other. In most cases, this is true and the bond between sisters is strong. Sisters share a history and a household that connects them. There may be issues, though, if there is a substantial age difference or if one daughter is preferred over another. Of course, family dynamics shape who we are and how we function within the family. Dysfunctional family systems serve to distort our image of self and our images of other family members. Sometimes sisters who have been estranged when young find meaningful ways to connect in adulthood.

Food for Thought

1. Do you have sisters? What is your relationship with them? Are there things you'd like to change about your relationships with your sisters?

2. Have you ever found yourself in conflict with a sister or friend over a love interest? If so, what was the outcome of the situation? If not, how have you avoided this situation?

3. Do you think friends should have some ground rules to order the friendship? If so, what are some of the nonnegotiables?

4. Have you ever been competitive with a sister or good friend? What was the source of the competition? What was the outcome of the situation?

5. Do you think Leah and Rachel ever resolved their issues with each other? Why or why not? What could Jacob have done to help the relationship between the two sisters?

Films and Television Shows

The Color Purple (1985) is based on a novel by Alice Walker. The film, set in the early 1900s, is about the life and journey of Celie (Whoopi Goldberg). Her life is filled with abuse, neglect, and pain. She is separated from her sister Nettie (Akosua Busia) and they promise to write each other until they are reunited. In her sister's absence, Celie writes letters to God and develops relationships with Shug (Margaret Avery), the mistress of Celie's husband, and Sofia (Oprah Winfrey), her stepdaughter-in-law. Celie never forgets her sister and lives in the hope that they will be reunited.

As you watch the film, pay attention to the relationships of the women.

- What is the nature of the relationship between Celie and Nettie? What holds them together?

- In what ways are Celie and Nettie like Leah and Rachel? How are they different from the biblical siblings?

- Under what circumstances do Celie and Shug meet? What is the nature of their relationship?

- What is the turning point of the film? How does this shape the rest of the film? What is the impact on Celie's female friendships?

- Sofia and Celie have a powerful confrontation. What is the outcome of this encounter?

- How do you interpret the ending of the film? Would you change anything about the ending?

Sister, Sister (1982) is written by Maya Angelou. The story is about Caroline (Diahann Carroll) and her sisters, Sissy (Irene Cara) and Frieda (Rosalind Cash), who are in the family home after their father dies. Caroline is the oldest daughter who stayed home and resents the turn her life has taken. Sissy is the youngest daughter who wants to live her own life. Frieda, the middle sister and single mother, left home, returns, seduces Caroline's boyfriend, and continues trying to find herself.

- Describe Caroline and her outlook on life. How does she reconcile her worldview with her affair with the minister? Does she resemble Leah or Rachel? In what ways?

- What is the nature of the relationship between Caroline and Frieda? What are the points of tension? What are the points of happiness?

- Is there a Jacob figure in the film? How does he interact with Caroline and Frieda? Explain your answer.

- What do you think happens to Sissy? What happens to Frieda's son?

- What moral issues do the sisters struggle over? How are their differences resolved?

Fatal Attraction (1987) is a classic film that deals with infidelity. It is not a film about sisters but it is the story about two women and their relationships with the same man. The film is based on a short film by James Dearden. The feature film is about Dan (Michael Douglas), a lawyer who is happily married to Beth (Anne Archer). One weekend, Dan has an affair with a business acquaintance, publishing company editor Alexandra (Glenn Close). Alexandra goes to great lengths to keep Dan in her life, to the point where she becomes obsessed with him.

Alexandra takes Dan on a roller coaster ride—she stalks him and phones him constantly. She tells him that she is pregnant, plans to keep the child, and tells him that he must take responsibility. All the while, Dan tries to keep the situation from his wife. Only near the end of the film does Dan confess to Beth, and Alexandra meets an unhappy end.

As you watch the film, pay attention to how the women are treated by Dan.

- Why does Dan have an affair with Alexandra? What are her expectations from their encounter?

- In what ways does Dan resemble Jacob? Explain.

- Does the relationship between Dan and Beth change? In what ways?

- Under what circumstances do Alexandra and Beth meet? How do you react to this scene? Are there similarities between this encounter and those we find between Rachel and Leah?

- What is the turning point in the film? How does the turning point shape the rest of the film?

- How do you feel about the treatment of Alexandra by Dan? By the writers and director of the film? Who ultimately pays for the adultery in this film? Explain your answer.

My Best Friend's Wedding (1997) is a rather typical romantic comedy. Julianne (Julia Roberts) is a successful food critic who has been good friends with Michael (Dermot Mulroney) since college. They made a pact that if neither had found their soul mate by the time they were twenty-eight, they'd marry each other. Just days before her twenty-eighth birthday, Julianne receives a call from Michael. He tells her that he has met the love of his life and plans to marry Kimberly (Cameron Diaz), a young college student from a wealthy family.

When Julianne realizes that she is in love with Michael, she goes to Chicago to stop the wedding. Her schemes do not work. In fact, Kimberly asks Julianne to be her maid of honor at the wedding. Julianne pretends to be a committed maid of honor but does all she can to sabotage the wedding. Finally, on the day of the wedding, she confesses to Michael how she feels about him.

As you watch the film, pay attention to the relationship between Julianne and Kimberly.

- Are there parallels between the biblical story and the film? Explain.

- Why does Kimberly ask Julianne to be her maid of honor? Why does Julianne accept?

- Why doesn't Julianne tell Michael how she feels as soon as she learns he's engaged to someone else?

- What is the turning point in the film? How does this influence the rest of the film?

- What advice do you think Leah would offer Julianne about her relationship to Michael? What advice do you think she'd offer Julianne about her relationship to Kimberly?

- How do you feel about the ending? Would you change it? If so, what ending would you prefer?

3

SHIPHRAH AND PUAH

Although we don't know much about their background, we know that these two women work together to save a nation. When women cooperate, they can confound and defy imperial power. In some ways, their collaborative effort leaves us laughing at the Egyptian Pharaoh.

Read
Exodus 1:8–22

The Back Story
The book of Exodus is about the liberation of a people who go on to form a nation. This book is pivotal because the people come to know God as Creator and Redeemer. God hears the cries of the oppressed Hebrews and frees them from oppression and frees them for community and nationhood.

We learn about Shiphrah and Puah because of Moses; their story is part of the larger text about Moses, the strong and clever leader who works with God to free the Hebrews from bondage in Egypt. But before we learn about him, we meet these two midwives.

The Hebrews had migrated to Egypt during a widespread famine throughout the Middle East in the lifetime of Joseph (first-born of Rachel, from our previous chapter). The people have done well—they have multiplied and been fruitful, just as God promised (see Gen. 1:28a). But when the leadership changes in Egypt, life for the Hebrews takes a curious turn. Instead of ease in Egypt, the people are confronted with an Egyptian ruler who does not know or care about Joseph and his ancestors. For the new Pharaoh, the Hebrews represent free labor—just another group of slaves to do all the work. All too soon Pharaoh also sees this numerous people as a threat to his power.

The Episode

Pharoah feels the need to control the Hebrews; he is afraid they will outnumber the Egyptians and fight against them should Egypt be attacked by an enemy. He has no way of knowing what the Hebrews will do, but he decides to take matters into his own hands and find a way to keep them under his control. He uses his imperial authority and power to slow down the population explosion of the enslaved Hebrews. His first effort is to force the people into hard labor building storehouses. Pharaoh mistakenly thought the people would be too exhausted from their labors to continue producing offspring. The Hebrews, indeed, work hard but they also continue having babies. Pharoah's second effort is commanding the midwives to kill Hebrew boys as soon as they are delivered. Again, the ruler mistakenly thinks that killing the males will slow the population growth of the Hebrews. This tactic might have worked, but the women undermine his efforts.

Instead of killing the baby boys, the midwives let them live. The two who are named in the Exodus narrative—Shiphrah and Puah—are specifically told to kill the boys (see Exod. 1:16). When the ruler realizes what is happening, he summons these two women for questioning. The women defend themselves by stating that the Hebrew women are strong and deliver their babies before the midwives arrive. They refuse to kill the babies after they are born. Interestingly, the ruler accepts their defense. He does not question them further and does not conduct his own investigation.

Instead, he moves to plan C: ordering every Egyptian to kill Hebrew boys under the age of two by tossing them into the Nile River. He is foiled again and is outraged that he can do nothing to stop the growth of the Hebrew people.

In the meantime, the midwives go about their business of assisting women in childbirth. In many cultures even today, women deliver their babies at home in the presence of midwives. Midwives are experienced assistants; they know what to do in cases of emergency and during difficult deliveries. They are important members of the community and are trusted to do what is best in any situation. Their job is to help bring life into the world, not destroy it. Pharaoh's order to kill the baby boys goes against everything the midwives stand for—they are about life, not death. To be sure, many women died during childbirth and there were situations where babies could not be saved. But the midwife did everything she could to take care of mother and child.

In the text, Shiphrah and Puah do not speak to each other. We don't know their motivations for defying the orders of the ruler. We don't see them in conversation and we don't know what they are thinking. What we know is that they "fear" God; that is, they revere God and believe that obeying God is better than obeying a human ruler.[1] Although the Egyptians often held their rulers up as gods, Shiphrah and Puah recognize a power greater than the ruler. And they are rewarded for their work on behalf of God— they thrive in their work and have strong families of their own.

Shiphrah and Puah are role models for collaboration and cooperation. They stand in their truth and practice what they preach—at the great risk to their own lives. They go against royal power and authority and remain true to their profession and to God. They work together to make something positive happen. Because of Shiphrah and Puah, a good number of Hebrew boys lived, including Moses.

The Contemporary Connection

The story of Shiphrah and Puah illustrates what happens when women take charge. This is an instance in the Bible where we find women working in tandem to make something positive happen. While we don't know much about these two midwives, we know that they feared God and protected life as a vocation. In many cases, women are able to come together around issues that affect their families.

However, women and people uniting around familial issues can have its shadow side, too. For instance, the civil rights movement was launched by African Americans to end racial discrimination in all areas of the society. The aims of the movement were racial pride, economic and political self-determination, and quality education for all. As blacks sought to desegregate public schools, they encountered angry crowds trying to keep black children from entering schools. The picture of white mothers shouting racial epithets, spitting and throwing things at buses holding black children is an ugly blot on our nation's history. We have come a long way from that period, but the scars remain and vestiges of racism continue to haunt us.

Women have more power collectively than when working alone. Historically, women in collaboration have addressed such issues as slavery, childcare, voting rights, reproductive rights, workplace concerns (wages, benefits, harassment), domestic violence and violation, and more. Collaboration has brought social, cultural, political, and religious change and greater freedom for women. For example, middle-class African American women worked together to put a spotlight on the lynching of men, women, and children in the early 1900s and engaged the government to end the practice. Likewise, mothers banded together to put a spotlight on drunken driving, and Mothers Against Drunk Driving (MADD) was formed and continues to raise awareness today.

It is important to note that some of these collaborations did not result, necessarily, in best friendships. Working together for a common cause can lead to such relationships, but achieving a goal is the focus. There is room for both kinds of relationships, and we can benefit from working with other women to better the world.

More and more, we see women cooperating in film and television. Films like *9 to 5* (1980, starring Jane Fonda, Lily Tomlin, and Dolly Parton) and *Norma Rae* (1979, starring Sally Field) dramatize the power of strong women focused on one goal. The goal might be to empower each other or to change public policy. Whatever the reasons for collaboration and cooperation, there is power in numbers, and women continue to work together to bring about change.

Food for Thought

1. In what ways does God act as a midwife? How does the fear of God empower Shiphrah and Puah to defy Pharaoh's order to kill male newborns?

2. Childbirth still presents challenges for women around the globe. What are some of those challenges? What kind of relationship is most helpful between mother and midwife?

3. How do you think Shiphrah and Puah dealt with fear? How do you deal with fear? How do you overcome fear so that you can move ahead?

4. Why do women have a difficult time working together? What have been your experiences of collaborating and cooperating with other women?

5. How can women overcome the difficulties of race and class so that they can collaborate? What kinds of issues draw women into circles of activism?

Films and Television Shows

Thelma and Louise (1991) is a well-known film and a prime example of what happens when women take off on their own. Thelma (Geena Davis) and Louise (Susan Sarandon) star in this female road-trip adventure. They both want to escape from the confinements of their lives. What starts off as an innocent excursion turns ominous and the women start running for their lives and away from the law. What they encounter in a Thunderbird convertible makes us laugh, cry, and reach for the tissues. They discover the meaning of friendship and find strength they didn't know they possessed.

As you watch the film, consider these questions.

- What is the nature of Thelma and Louise's friendship? Why do they decide to take a road trip?

- In what ways do Thelma and Louise mirror Shiphrah and Puah?

- What do you think haunts the two women in the film? What is missing from their lives?

- Describe the men the two leave behind. Describe the men they meet on the road.

- What does each woman learn about herself during this adventure? How does their friendship empower each woman?

- How do you feel about the ending of the film? What changes would you make?

I Love Lucy (1951–1957; available on DVD) is an early sitcom (situation comedy) set in New York. The plot revolves around the lives of Lucy Ricardo (Lucille Ball), her singer-entertainer husband Ricky Ricardo (Desi Arnaz), and their neighbor-landlords Fred (William Frawley) and Ethel (Vivian Vance) Mertz. Lucy and Ethel epitomize the perfect duo for wacky adventures. Lucy's ambition to be a show business star leads her into some improbable situations and she draws Ethel into her antics despite Ethel's initial resistance. The fact that she has no talent does not keep Lucy from putting herself out there. The friendship between Lucy and Ethel takes them on adventures where they shake up the status quo.

As you watch episodes of the show, consider these questions.

- What is the nature of Lucy and Ethel's friendship?
- What motivates Lucy to do what she does? In what ways does Ethel support and even encourage Lucy's adventures?
- In what ways does the pair use their power in subversive ways to get what they want? How do the men react to them? How do the relationships parallel those in the Shiphrah and Puah story?
- How does Lucy deal with the objections of her husband? In what ways are her tactics outdated?
- Do you have a friend with whom you do wild or wacky things? What kinds of adventures have you had with your girlfriends?

Cagney and Lacey (1982–1988 and available on DVD; visit the official website http://www.cagneyandlacey.com/) is a police drama series that focuses on the female team of Christine Cagney (Sharon Gless) and Mary Beth Lacey (Tyne Daly). The women deal with their differences: Christine is single and fully invested in her career while Mary Beth is married with children. They bring to the screen various professional and personal issues women face in the workplace. The women find creative and edgy ways to deal with men in a traditionally male-dominated field. The show was created by former best friends Barbara Avedon and Barbara Corday.

As you watch episodes of the show, consider the following questions.

- In what ways are Cagney and Lacey different? In what ways are they the same?
- What does the show imply about women in traditionally male professions? How do Cagney and Lacey defy stereotypes as women?
- In what ways do the women support and affirm each other? In what ways do they challenge each other?
- What do you think Shiphrah and Puah would admire about Cagney and Lacey? What might the biblical woman question?
- What issues does the show highlight that women continue to battle?

Set It Off (1996) is set in a poor section of Los Angeles and centers on a group of friends who have all had some kind of run-in with authority figures or the police. They all need money for various reasons and decide to rob banks. Francesca, a.k.a. Frankie (Vivica A. Fox), loses her job at a bank because bank officials think she had something to do with a random robbery. Lita, a.k.a. Stoney (Jada Pinkett Smith), is devastated at the accidental shooting of her brother by the police; she wants a fresh start. Tisean, a.k.a. TT (Kimberly Elise), does not have childcare for her son; he accidentally ingests cleaning solution while on the job with TT and child protective services take the child into custody. Cleopatra, a.k.a. Cleo (Queen Latifah), wants money to bankroll her lifestyle of partying and drinking. Each woman has been mistreated by personal friends, acquaintances, and social systems. They deal with each other's weaknesses and foibles while learning to trust each other. They share their hopes and dreams and consider themselves a contemporary Robin Hood gang—all for one and one for all. This is a modern-day film that reminds us that right and wrong are not always very simple and that there are a number of ways to use one's power.

As you watch the film, consider the following questions.

- In what ways are all four women victims? In what ways are they victors?

- Who are the oppressors of the women in the film? In what ways are the men in the film mirror images of Pharaoh we see in the biblical text?

- Consider the rooftop scene early in the film. What holds the four friends together?

- How do you feel about their activity as bank robbers? Do you condemn them or empathize with them?

- What would Shiphrah and Puah admire about the women? What might they question?

- Do you think these women are considered heroes in their old neighborhood? Explain.

4

JEPHTHAH'S DAUGHTER AND HER COMPANIONS

Poor daughter—she is not named in the Bible and becomes the sacrificial offering because of her father's vow. But she takes control of the situation even though she knows she will die. Her friends gather with her in ritual to mark her death.

Read

Judges 11:34–40

The Back Story

The Book of Judges describes biblical life before the first monarch was called to rule over Israel. At the time, Israel is a loose federation of tribes that comes together when needed. The period is marked by a pattern: a time of relative peace and prosperity, a turning away from God during the good times, the threat of and oppression by a stronger nation, a time of repentance and crying to God for help, the rise of a charismatic military leader, success against the military threat and oppression, and a time of relative peace and prosperity. The pattern is repeated on a fairly regular basis. The charismatic leader is called a "judge." The judge is raised up by God, who bestows power and authority. Because of the divine call and blessing, the judge is able to rally the tribes for a particular purpose. Israel does not yet have an infrastructure or bureaucracy and thus no standing army. The tribes depend on each other to help out in times of trouble. The judge, then, is the answer to the people's cry for help. The judge is raised up to get a job done; when that job is done, the judge fades into the background or disappears from the text altogether.

Israel is led by twelve judges—eleven men and one woman.[1] Each judge is evaluated by how faithfully s/he walks in the ways of God. The two judges who do not walk in the ways of God experience personal tragedy: Samson dies a painful death and Jephthah loses his only child.

Military threats and subsequent domination were seen as vehicles of God sent to punish the Israelites for faithlessness within the community. During trying times, the people confess their sinfulness and seek help from God. It is not surprising that the Israelites have a difficult time settling in the land of Canaan. There were already several groups of people occupying the land. They did not roll over and let the Israelites take over their territories; instead, they fought to hold on to the lands they felt were legitimately theirs. And the situation was not all about clearing the land of other people. The Israelites tried to peacefully co-exist with their neighbors and some even assimilated into other cultures. When this happened, the people turned away from their one true God to worship other gods, a definite no-no for them. Their apostasy had an impact on their relationships with their neighbors. In Judges 11, the military threat is from Ammon. The Ammonites threaten the territory of Gilead and its capital city, Mizpah. The residents of Gilead know they need a strong leader to ward off the Ammonites, and they call upon Jephthah.

Jephthah is an interesting character. His mother is a prostitute who is not named in the text. His father marries another woman and has more children. The sons, Jephthah's half brothers, run Jephthah out of town, just in case he had any ideas about trying to cash in on an inheritance when their father dies. Jephthah soon is the leader of a gang of outlaws; he distinguishes himself as a shrewd and clever warrior. In every way, Jephthah is an outsider—he is an "outside" child who is run "outside" his hometown. His only friends are "outsiders." Yet when times get hard, his former kinsfolk ask him to come home.

When elders from his hometown ask him to lead the fight against the Ammonites, Jephthah resists. His response doesn't hide his anger and hurt; they basically ask him to let bygones be bygones. He negotiates a deal with them—if he is successful, he will become the permanent leader in Gilead. Jephthah convinces them that any victory he claims will be due to God's help and blessing. The elders agree and offer Jephthah the job (see Judg. 11:11). That Jephthah negotiates a deal to become permanent leader speaks to his ambition and possibly his need to get back at his hometown folks for allowing him to be exiled from his community. Throughout much of the Hebrew Bible and certainly in the Book of Judges, military leaders are raised up and anointed by God; they are temporary leaders only. That Jephthah strikes a deal to assume permanent leadership is a clue that something ominous will happen, even though he cloaks his ambition in God-language. If he is successful against the Ammonites, it is only because God wills it to be so; at least, that is what he says. We'll see.

Jephthah tries to negotiate a deal with the Ammonites. This is an instance where a reasonable compromise is preferable to war. But his offers are rejected. The Ammonite leader says that Israel took land between Arnon and Jabbok that was not theirs to take; the territory was given to the tribes of Reuben and Gad. Jephthah denies the claim: in order for the Israelites to get to the promised land, they needed to pass through Edom and Moab. Neither nation granted access and the Israelites were forced to pass through the land of the Amorites. The Amorites also denied access and attacked Israel without just cause. God allowed Israel to defeat the Amorites and the Israelites settled there. The land actually belonged to the Ammonites, but it was too late—Israel laid claim to the land. The Ammonites refute Jephthah's argument. He tries again by stating that the Ammonite god, Chemosh, had a chance to save the land for the Ammonites but did not. Jephthah's God prevailed and there is no need for war now since the incident happened three hundred years ago (see Judg. 11:12–28). Jephthah realizes that he has no choice but to go to war. God anoints him—the first time God acts in this episode and ensures a victory. On top of God's actions, Jephthah vows to give a burnt offering to God *if* God will bless him with a victory. Jephthah's vow is redundant and unnecessary. We are not sure why he offers the vow; is he showing off in front of his kinsfolk? Is this a sign of genuine faith and hope? Is he engaging in hyperbole because he has an audience? We cannot be sure what his motives are. All we know is that he is victorious. We prepare for a horrifying story to unfold.

The Episode

This is one of the most haunting stories in the Bible. An innocent young woman is put to death by her father. She is placed in an impossible situation. The poor woman of this story doesn't even have a name. Her identity is tied to her father and his actions, which bring about her death. Yet she is able to chart her fate even within patriarchal limitations so that she is not forgotten.

Jephthah's vow, to sacrifice the first person who comes out of his house to meet him, is binding and cannot be revoked or changed (see Deut. 23:21–23). Biblical scholars are divided on whether Jephthah intends to make a human or animal sacrifice. He intends to burn someone or something as an offering to God. Jephthah marches off to war after enlisting help from Manasseh.

His military campaign is stated in a matter-of-fact manner: he "inflicted a massive defeat." The Ammonites are crushed. Jephthah is a hero—hometown boy makes good and all is right with the world. At least, for the time being. Jephthah goes home to Mizpah to continue his celebration. Only his celebration is short-lived. The first person to emerge from his house is his daughter! The text underscores the impending dread—she is his only child, there are none besides her (see Judg. 11:34c). His jubilation turns to despair as he tears his clothes as a sign of grief.

Jephthah's vow requires him to execute his daughter, his virgin child. To make matters worse, Jephthah blames her for what he must do (see Judg. 11:35b). He manages to make this tragic situation about him, not her. He must fulfill the vow. He has no choice. We expect her to put up a fight and get her father to change his mind. We expect her to weep and wail, maybe even run away to escape the hands of her father. We expect her to plead for her life or suggest a viable substitute. She not only accepts her fate but also comforts her father (see Judg. 11:36).

She makes one last request: to have two months alone with her girlfriends. In her last days, she turns to her friends for comfort and the space to accept the inevitable. She gathers young women to help her prepare for death. They mourn with her, no doubt grieving what she will miss—marriage, children, and grandchildren. She displays a strong will—although she has no choice about whether she dies, she determines the time.

She is not saved at the last minute like Isaac (see Gen. 22:9–14). Her life is prematurely snuffed out by the hand of her father. His life goes on but hers is ended. She dies a needless death but she does so heroically. The only comfort in this episode is the action of her friends.

In her moments of greatest need, Jephthah's daughter is surrounded by her friends. It is up to them to keep her memory alive and they do so in ritual. Each year, the women gather for four days to remember her—likely by song, prayers, stories past, and stories about what could have been. Jephthah's daughter is alive because the women keep her alive. Their memory of her is a testimony to the courage she displayed in the face of death.

Jephthah bemoans his daughter's fate but seems more concerned about how her death affected him than how it affected her. After she returned from her time of mourning, he moved along with his life. He continued to fight battles and led the people of Gilead. He faded from history, but his daughter was remembered and her life celebrated long after his died. Thank God for the women who refused to let their friend's life be in vain.

The Contemporary Connection

Popular culture is filled with films that portray the brevity of life and how friends help the transition to death. Through thick and thin, women rally together when they are needed. Whether one's transition is sudden or lingering, a good friend can help just by being there.

In her time of greatest need, Jephthah's daughter depended on her friends to help her face death. Friends are there for us when we face disaster; they help us make lemonade out of lemons. Our closest friends help us come to grips with reality, no matter how bleak.

Jephthah's daughter gathered with her friends so she could die a "good" death—with grace and the assurance that death is not the last word for anyone. She wanted a time to say goodbye. Despite her father's foolish vow, she had the power to say "no, I need some time with my girls!" She claimed her power to determine when she would die, and her friends supported her. They surrounded her with their companionship and ritualized their relationship even as they mourned the impending doom that awaited her.

Food for Thought

1. Describe what a best friend is to you. What do you need from a best friend? Are you willing and able to be a best friend to another woman? In what ways or why not?

2. Do you have girlfriends who will be there for you no matter what? Tell a story about one of them. How does your story parallel that of Jephthah's daughter and her friends? How does it differ?

3. In what ways and in what situations have your friends been there for you? If you don't have a friend who will stay the course with you, say how you feel about the absence of such a friend.

4. Have you ever failed to be there for a friend who needed you? What was the outcome of the situation? Were you able to make it up to her? Were you forgiven? Have you forgiven yourself?

5. Are there limits to what you are willing to share with your closest friends? What are those limits?

Films and Television Shows

Sex and the City (1998–2004; available on DVD; official website, http://www.hbo.com/sex-and-the-city/index.html) is the infamous television series that first aired on the cable station HBO. It chronicles the lives and adventures of four New York friends. The series stars newspaper columnist Carrie (Sarah Jessica Parker), ambitious attorney Miranda (Cynthia Nixon), naïve art gallery manager Charlotte (Kristin Davis), and public relations expert and sexually uninhibited Samantha (Kim Cattrall). *Be warned: many episodes of the series are explicit and not for the sensitive; there are graphic sexual scenes and much foul language.* Still, the show gives us inside glimpses into the friendships that give meaning to the lives of these women. In fact, except for Miranda, none of them seem to have siblings or family other than each other. In one episode, Miranda's mother dies and we see (ever so briefly) her siblings. Since its cancellation on television, the creators have made two films, *Sex and the City 1* and *2*, to further explore the lives of these four friends. Together the women weather the joys and pain of life and love.

As you view episodes of the series, consider these questions.

- What draws these four women together? How do you suppose they met?

- In what ways do they challenge each other to think differently about themselves and their lives?

- In what ways do they support and affirm each other? How do they settle disagreements?

- In what ways do the women in the show illustrate and embody the friendship between Jephthah's daughter and her friends?

- What topics and areas of life does the series deal with? Are any topics off limits for these friends?

Boys on the Side (1995) is a film about three women who are there for each other during trying times. The plot revolves around Robin (Mary-Louise Parker), a real estate agent who is looking for a traveling companion to drive with her cross country from New York to California. She places an ad in a paper and Jane (Whoopi Goldberg) answers. Jane is a lounge singer who is looking for a fresh start after a romance ends. On the way, they stop in Pittsburgh to take Holly (Drew Barrymore), Robin's friend, to lunch. While in Pittsburgh, Robin and Jane discover that Holly is being physically abused by her boyfriend, and they invite her to join them on the drive to California. This is a road trip film with a twist—each woman is running away from something without a clear vision of what she is running toward. Robin is HIV positive; Jane is a lesbian; and Holly is pregnant. Their sharing bonds them together as they deal with differences, joys, and tragedy.

As you watch the film, consider the following questions.

- How do Robin and Jane establish their relationship? What secrets does each woman withhold from the other?

- How does Robin react to Holly's situation? Are there options that should have been explored before Holly took matters into her own hands?
- What advice do you think Jephthah's daughter might offer to each of the women in the film?
- What is the turning point of the film? How does this shape the ways in which the friendship among the three women develops?
- What does the title of the film, *Boys on the Side,* mean?
- How do you think the characters' lives would unfold beyond the film?

Girlfriends (2000–2008; available on DVD, sometimes runs in syndication) is a sitcom that deals with the lives, loves, and mishaps of four best friends. The four African American characters are attorney-turned-restaurateur Joan (Tracee Ellis Ross), real estate agent and broker Toni (Jill Marie Jones), former administrative assistant, now self-help author Maya (Golden Brooks), and free spirit turned musician Lynn (Persia White). Set in Los Angeles, the show raised issues of race, class, professional ambition, sexuality, romance, marriage, infidelity, divorce, childrearing, miscarriage, dysfunctional families, competition, conflict, and loss. Although the show is a comedy, there is heavy drama in many of the episodes.

As you watch episodes of the show, consider the following questions.

- What is the glue that holds the four women together as friends?
- How do the women deal with each other's foibles? Are the scenarios realistic?
- How do Joan and Toni deal with their conflicts? What advice would Jephthah's daughter offer the two about life, love, and friendship?

- The four women are different: Joan is wealthy but plays it down; Maya is a working-class woman from Compton; Toni is a materialistic snob; and Lynn is a biracial sexually uninhibited woman who is chronically un/underemployed. How do the women deal with their differences?

- In what ways do they exhibit love, care, and compassion for each other?

- Would you want any of these women to be your friend? Why or why not?

Waiting to Exhale (1995) is based on the novel by Terry McMillan and directed by actor Forest Whitaker. The plot revolves around the lives of four friends who live in Phoenix. Each is waiting for her life to fall into place so she can "exhale." The characters are television producer Savannah (Whitney Houston), homemaker and divorcee Bernadine (Angela Bassett), ambitious business executive Robin (Lela Rochon), and beauty salon owner and single mother Gloria (Loretta Devine). The women, upper-middle class, have all kinds of issues, mostly related to men. Savannah is involved with a married man; Bernadine's husband leaves her for a white woman; Robin is also involved with a married man; and Gloria is overweight and is reluctant to let her son leave home.

As you watch the film, consider the following questions.

- What is the relationship like between Savannah and her mother? In what ways do they support each other?

- What kind of relationship do you think Jephthah's daughter had with her own mother? Explain.

- What holds the four women together as friends? How do they support each other? How do they challenge each other?

- What is the turning point of the film? How does this shape the relationships among the women?

- Do any of the women exhale? In what ways? In what ways are they still holding their breath?

- What advice do you think Jephthah's daughter would offer the women about life?

The Sisterhood of the Traveling Pants (2005) is based on the young adult novel of the same title by Anne Brashares. The story is about four best friends living in Bethesda, Maryland, who want to stay connected over the summer while each is off on her own adventure. They find and buy a pair of secondhand jeans that happens to fit them all perfectly despite their differing body types. They pass the jeans around, along with an update on their activities. The friends are Lena (Alexis Bledel), who travels with her grandparents to Greece for the summer; Tibby (Amber Tamblyn), who is staying in Maryland for the summer and makes a film; Bridget (Blake Lively), who travels to Mexico for soccer camp; and Carmen (America Ferrera), who travels to South Carolina to visit her father. As you watch the film, consider the following questions.

- What draws the four young women together? Describe their friendship.

- What connections do you make between the four young women in the film and the biblical story of Jephthah's daughter and her friends?

- How do the traveling pants keep the friends connected? Are there ways in which the pants symbolize the annual ritual the friends of Jephthah's daughter hold for her? Explain your answer.

- The friends show maturity beyond their years. How do they become so wise?

- In what ways were their adventures similar? How do the adventures deepen the friendship among the young women?

5

R U T H   A N D   N A O M I

This story of a daughter and mother-in-law defies the popular cultural portrayal of women at odds over a man.

Read
Ruth 1:16–18

The Back Story
Widows are a class of women in the biblical world who were of special concern. Widows typically did not inherit their husband's estates, which usually went to their sons. Sons were obligated to take care of their mothers; in cases where there were no sons or daughters, widows were often broke and homeless. Israelites were encouraged to care for widows (and orphans) by providing for their needs (see Deut. 25:5–10; Isa. 1:17; Jer. 7:5–7). Still, widows were subject to exploitation, abuse, and neglect. Widows were among the most vulnerable members of the community. Widows, having few rights, were left to their own devices, and their futures were very much at risk.

Even so, the Bible makes it clear that God cared for the lives and prospects of widows. The Hebrew prophets called for community care and compassion for widows, and Jesus expressed concern for widows. Most often, widows were marginalized in the Bible. Too often, widows struggled to make a life for themselves and went to great lengths to take care of themselves.

The Episode

The Book of Ruth tells the story of Naomi and her daughter-in-law Ruth, who are both widows. Their journey is one of struggles and surprising developments. Naomi is married to Elimelech, and they have two sons, Mahlon and Chilion. They moved from Bethlehem to Moab seeking food during a famine. After Elimelech died, the sons married Moabite women: Mahlon married Ruth and Chilion married Orpah. Ten years later, at the time of our story, Mahlon and Chilion die before they have had children. Now, all three women are childless and widowed.

Naomi decides to return to Bethlehem and encourages her daughters-in-law to stay in Moab. They are to return to their mothers' houses. The younger women are reluctant to leave Naomi, but her argument is convincing—perhaps they will fare better than she. God has given her a hard blow that leaves her husbandless and childless. With any luck, the younger women will marry and have children. Such will not be the case for Naomi, she states. Naomi blesses the women and says goodbye in the midst of tears and sorrow. Orpah goes to her mother's house. But Ruth refuses; she decides to stay with Naomi, no matter what.

Upon their arrival in Bethlehem, Naomi is honest about her situation—she is poor, widowed, with few prospects for a happy future. She has returned home with nothing and cannot see anything in the days ahead to relieve her misery. Ruth refuses to give up and does whatever she can to put food on the table, including gleaning the fields of Boaz, a well-to-do Israelite and distant relative of Naomi. Because of Ruth's loyalty to Naomi, Boaz has pity on her and helps her out (see Ruth 2:8–13). When she shares the bounty with Naomi, the elder woman asks Ruth what happened. When Ruth shares the story of meeting Boaz, Naomi hatches a plan to ensure that Boaz marries Ruth, thereby guaranteeing a future for both women (see Ruth 3). The plan requires Ruth to trust Naomi fully, and she does as she is instructed. Boaz proves an honorable man and settles things between the next closest kin, Naomi, and himself. In this way, he acquires the land that belonged to Elimelech as well as responsibility for his household. He marries Ruth.

Ruth and Boaz have a son. The women of Bethlehem praise Naomi because she has been redeemed from poverty and destitution—see Ruth 4:14–17. The women of the neighborhood name the child Obed; his son is named Jesse and Jesse's son is named David, the great ruler of Israel and ancestor of Jesus.

The story of Naomi and Ruth is a story of love and loyalty. They redefine family and claim their kinship with each other. The older Naomi is wise and has much to teach Ruth about life and the ways of women. They do not let cultural prejudices separate them. The blending of Israelite and Moabite families is testament to the mixing of nationalities in biblical times. The bond between the two women is so strong that Ruth is willing to give up everything to follow Naomi. She is willing to learn how to fit into a new culture and to take on a new religion to stay with her mother-in-law. She is willing to embrace a new life.

The Contemporary Connection

It is almost a cliché that there will be problems between mothers and their sons' wives. Such moms are the brunt of many a stand-up comic's routine. The stereotype of the clinging mom who loves her son to the point where no woman is good enough for him is just that—a stereotype. But it is one that has a hard time dying.

The mom is blamed for all the weaknesses in her son—and the son is mocked as a "mama's boy."

The story of Naomi and Ruth certainly defies the stereotype. Instead, we find a woman who loves her daughters-in-law and treats them well. As a daughter-in-law herself, perhaps Naomi understands the difficulty some mothers have in letting their children grow and lead their own lives. Perhaps Naomi had a difficult mother-in-law. Or perhaps hers was a stellar role model on how to get along with extended family. Or perhaps Naomi understands that her faith calls for inclusive welcome and kinship regardless of background and culture.

At any rate, we find that Naomi and Ruth have a loving, respectful relationship filled with trust and compassion. The women work together to ensure their future—it's all for one and one for all. And it's a family affair.

Food for Thought

1. If you are married, what is your relationship like with your mother-in-law? Have things changed over time? In what ways?

2. If you are not married, have you met the mother of any of your significant others? Describe your relationship with her.

3. If you are a mother-in-law, how do you differ from your own? How would your daughter-in-law describe your relationship?

4. Describe the ideal mother/daughter-in-law relationship. What are the positives? How do the two women in these roles work to overcome challenges?

5. What advice would Ruth and Naomi offer today's mothers-in-law? What would they say to daughters-in-law today?

6. Do you have friendships with women who are significantly younger or older than you? Describe those relationships. How are they different from friendships with your peers?

Films and Television Shows

Hush (1998) is a thriller-suspense film about Martha (Jessica Lange), who loves her son, Jackson (Jonathon Schaech). Jackson brings home his fiancé, Helen (Gwyneth Paltrow), to meet mom. Martha wants Jackson to come home and run the horse farm. Jackson and Helen love living in New York and are not ready to give up city life. When Helen becomes pregnant, she and Jackson marry and move to the horse farm. The controlling Martha has a secret that will shatter the lives of the newlyweds. Martha's mother-in-law, Alice (Nina Foch), is kept in a nursing home for fear that she will reveal the secret that Martha has been holding since Jackson's childhood.

As you watch the film, consider the following questions.

- Under what circumstances do Martha and Helen meet? How do they react to each other?

- Describe the relationship between Martha and Alice. How is their relationship similar to and different from that between Martha and Helen?

- What stereotypical mother-in-law elements do you find in the film? In what ways does the biblical story challenge the stereotypes in the film?

- What are your feelings about Jackson and Helen's wedding?

- What is the turning point of the film? How does this shape the rest of the film?

- Is there any possibility for Martha and Helen to establish a healthy relationship? Why or why not?

Eve's Bayou (1997), directed by Kasi Lemmons, is a multilayered film about family—sisters, in-laws, and all the drama that happens in an upper-class Louisiana household. The Batiste family is headed by the charming Louis (Samuel L. Jackson), who is the neighborhood doctor. He has a roaming eye that his wife, Roz (Lynn Whitfield), conveniently overlooks. His daughter, Eve (Junee Smollett), however, does not ignore it and shares her suspicions with her older sister, Cisely (Meagan Good). The sisters share a deep bond despite Eve's feelings of jealousy at the relationship between Cisely and their father. Roz shares a bond with her sister-in-law Mozelle (Debbie Morgan) and they support each other unconditionally. Louis and Mozelle's mother, Gran Mere (Ethel Ayler), lives in the Batiste family home and offers her opinion on a variety of subjects. There are many secrets in the Batiste family and it is not clear what is truth and what is fiction.

As you watch the film, consider the following questions.

- Describe the relationship between Eve and Cisely. What are the tensions in their relationship?

- Describe the relationship between Roz and Mozelle. What holds them together? How do they support each other?

- What role does Gran Mere play in the household? Are there connections between her presence in the home and the biblical story? What are they? How are they illustrated in the film?

- What secret do Eve and Cisely share? What is the truth about their secret?

The Golden Girls (1985–1992) is a sitcom about four older women living under the same roof in Miami, Florida. The series starred Bea Arthur as the divorced Dorothy, a substitute teacher; Estelle Getty as the widowed Sophia, Dorothy's mother, who is homeless after her retirement home burned down; Rue McClanahan as the widowed Blanche, the ultimate Southern belle, who worked at an art gallery; and Betty White as the widowed Rose, the dimwitted but often wise one, who worked as a grief counselor. Dorothy and Rose respond to Blanche's ad for housemates and later Sophia moves in. No topic is off limits for this group of uninhibited women—love and romance, sex after age fifty, menopause, aging, finances, dealing with children, dealing with aging parents, competition with other women, forgiveness, jealousy, insecurity, elder care, and other issues.

As you watch the show, consider the following questions.

- How did these women become friends? What holds them together?

- How do they communicate with each? In what ways do they affirm each other? In what ways do they empower each other?

- How do they handle disagreements? What can you learn from them about communication?

- In what ways does the show mirror the biblical story? In what ways does the show differ from the story of Ruth and Naomi? How are men treated in the show?

- In what ways is Sophia like a mother to all the women?

- Are the issues of the elderly very different from the issues of younger women? Explain.

6

HERODIAS AND
HER DAUGHTER

Mother-daughter relationships can be challenging. There are moments of closeness and moments of distance. Sometimes, moms want to hold on to their baby girls and protect them from the world. Sometimes, daughters are cruel in their attempts for independence. The bond between a mother and her daughter can be strong and healthy despite times of challenge.

Read
Mark 6:14–29

The Back Story
We meet Herodias and her daughter as part of the narrative about John the Baptist. The two women conspire to have John executed. We find their stories in the Gospels of Matthew (14:4–12) and Mark (6:14–29); Luke (9:7–9) states John's demise in a matter-of-fact man-

ner with few details. Scholars generally agree that Mark is the earliest of the three and that Matthew and Luke used Mark as the framework for their Gospels. We will focus on Mark's longer, richer telling.

We first meet John in Mark 1:4 where he is preaching and baptizing people in his wilderness ministry. He is like one of the Hebrew prophets—preaching with urgency that the reign of God is near and that people should repent and turn back to God. His ministry is the opening act to the appearance of Jesus of Nazareth. John is arrested in Mark 1:14 but we don't find out why until Mark 6.

John's arrest and subsequent execution is told as a flashback—Herod Antipas, the Roman governor of Galilee and Perea, comes from a long line of leaders, including his father, Herod the Great. John publicly condemns Herod Antipas for divorcing his first wife to marry Herodias. Herodias divorced her first husband, with whom she had a daughter, to marry Herod Antipas, her ex-husband's half brother and her half uncle. The historian Flavius Josephus, considered a reliable source, said that her first husband was Herod (whom Matthew and Mark identify as Philip) and states that her daughter's name was Salome. The Herod family tree is a tangled and layered one; Herod Antipas and Herodias are related in some way, which makes their marriage illegal according to Israelite custom and law (see Lev. 18:6–16; 20:21). John condemns the royal family. Herod Antipas takes the criticism in stride but his wife, Herodias, just can't let the matter go. Her grudge against John sets the stage for our Bible study.

The Episode

Herodias seems to have a bigger problem with John than does her husband. She is livid with John and wants to have him executed but she does not have the power to do so. Instead, Herod Antipas has John arrested and imprisoned. Herod Antipas believes John is a righteous and holy person; the Greek phrase implies that John is a person of utmost integrity and character. In fact, Herod Antipas holds John in high reverence and likes listening to him, even if he doesn't agree with John's message. Besides that, John is popular and the people like him; if he is executed, there is no telling how the people would react. Herod Antipas' job is to keep the peace and he cannot afford any riots or uprisings that John's murder might bring about. John the Baptist is quite the charismatic and fiery character—people come from miles around to hear his preaching. Herod Antipas is willing to let John languish in jail, but Herodias cannot let the matter go; she waits for an opportune time to get rid of John permanently.

The opportune time turns out to be Herod Antipas' birthday, when he holds a feast to celebrate. As he entertains his guests, he calls for Herodias' daughter to dance for them. Scholars find this curious because it would have been improper for the daughter to dance for her stepfather and his friends; she was a member of the royal family and such displays were frowned upon. However, she dances so well that Herod "promises on oath to grant her whatever she might ask." Perhaps he thought she would ask for an increase in her allowance or a shopping spree. Surely, he must have thought her request would be some innocent indulgence.

The young woman seeks the advice of her mother, who sees her chance for revenge. Mom is clear that her daughter should ask for nothing less than John's head on a platter. Although he is upset by the request, Herod Antipas grants her wish. It may be that he wants to save face in front of his friends, and, because of his oath, he is obligated to follow through on her request. John is beheaded and his head presented to the daughter, who in turn presents it to her mom.

The mother-daughter conspiracy leaves us breathless. We don't know the nature of their relationship. The daughter clearly respects her mother when she seeks her mother's advice on what to ask for from her stepfather. But the mother doesn't have her daughter's interest in mind; Herodias sees her own opportunity to be rid of the pesky John once and for all. She is portrayed as ruthless and vengeful. She uses her daughter to do her bidding—not exactly a good role model is Herodias. Unfortunately, we don't see her or her daughter in any other setting in the Bible. They are known by this episode in which an innocent person is executed.

The Contemporary Connection

There is not much in the biblical text to help us understand Herodias and her daughter. Our thinking about them has been influenced by the opera composed by Richard Strauss, *Salomé*. In the opera, Herodias and her daughter, Salomé, are women who use their womanly wiles to seduce and confuse men. Salomé performs the sensual dance of the seven veils, which prompts Herod Antipas to make his foolish oath. The opera uses poetic license to tell the story and we are influenced by it.

We are familiar with films and television programs that portray women as evil temptresses whose only goal in life is to destroy unknowing men. The portrayal of a mother and daughter team conniving against an innocent man fits in with popular beliefs that women cannot be trusted.

We cannot get a fuller picture of Herodias and Salome's relationship from the biblical texts. We see a young woman who seeks the wisdom of her mother. She gives her mother permission to tell her what to ask for; this is not likely the first time the daughter has sought her mother's counsel. We don't know if Herodias gave her daughter any instructions when Herod Antipas asked her to dance for his guests. So we cannot say what she might have advised her daughter, but a number of questions are raised. Did she teach her daughter how to dance? Was the dance a nice ballet or something more suggestive? Was the mother outraged over the request or did she remain silent? Did the daughter try to reason with her mother? Did they have prior conversations about John?

Herod Antipas seems comfortable asking the young woman, his stepdaughter, to entertain his friends where there is a lot of food and drink. The daughter displays no qualms about asking that an innocent man be executed. She is willing to have others kill for her mother. Perhaps their bond was so strong that the daughter was a mere puppet for her mom's vengeful desire.

Many films portray the extremes of the mother-daughter relationship. Either the women are best friends who support and confide in one another or they are rivals who hurt and harm each other. In some films, a mother and daughter may reach a point of understanding, but it's usually because of some catastrophic event that helps them realize that they actually love each other.

In real life, mother-daughter relationships tend to be more balanced. There may be ups and downs, but when daughters reach adulthood, they develop a different appreciation for their mothers. When daughters become mothers, their relationships with their own mothers can take a drastic turn for the better. In some families, though, a happy compromise may never be reached.

Conflicts and tensions may be inevitable. The child must test the boundaries and push them. Mothers must know when and how to let go so their children can grow and become self-sufficient. The balance is hard to reach and maintain. In healthy families, though, equilibrium is achieved and mutual respect can flourish.

Food for Thought

1. Describe your relationship with your own mother. Does the relationship provide what you believe you need? Share as much as you feel comfortable.

2. If you have a daughter, describe your relationship with her. If you have more than one, describe your relationship with each. How are your relationships with each different? What accounts for the differences? How would your daughter(s) describe her/their relationship(s) with you?

3. In what ways do women compete with each other, especially mothers and daughters?

4. How do you define "power?" Describe your power in relationships with women? In what ways do mothers and daughters exercise power in their relationship to each other? What accounts for the conflict that sometimes happens between mothers and daughters?

5. What values does Herodias pass along to her daughter? What are some lessons you've learned from your mother about friendships? What are some lessons you've learned from your daughter about friendships?

Films and Television Shows

Mommy Dearest (1981) is based on Christina Crawford's autobiography. Joan Crawford is unflatteringly depicted as an abusive mother who traumatizes her children. A major motion picture star, Joan (Faye Dunaway) is unable to have children and suffers a number of miscarriages before she adopts five children: Christina, Christopher I (who was reclaimed by his biological mother), Christopher II, Cathy, and Cynthia (the latter two twins). Despite her celebrity status, Joan makes unwise decisions about men, alcohol, and her career. Christina (Diana Scarwid) becomes the object of Joan's abuse. In the film, Joan is a controlling perfectionist who is obsessed with cleanliness. For the public eye, Joan dotes on Christina but behind the scene, she intimidates and heaps harsh discipline upon the child. Christina's rebellion is met with violence. Joan is unable or unwilling to reconcile with her daughter, and her daughter is unable or unwilling to forgive her mother. Of course, this is Christina's story; it would be interesting to read how Joan saw their relationship. Some now question how accurate Christina's childhood memories are; it is to be noted that her damaging book was written after Joan's death.

As you watch the film, consider the following questions.

- What was missing in Joan's life that she fulfilled by adopting children?

- Why is Christina so unhappy with her life? How truthful do you think she is in the telling of her life story?
- What kinds of tensions are likely between mothers and daughters? What can be done to avoid these tensions?
- What happens that leads to the scene and the now famous line, "No wire hangers ever!"?
- What could Joan and Christina learn from the biblical story? What could they teach Herodias and Salome?
- How does competition and jealousy play out in this mother-daughter relationship?
- Are there parallels between the film and the story of Herodias and her daughter? Name and explain them.

Terms of Endearment, (1983) is the adaptation of a novel by Larry McMurtry. Aurora (Shirley MacLaine) and Emma (Debra Winger) are a mother and daughter who both look for love in all the wrong places. After some ups and downs, Emma becomes ill. Although there have been tensions in their relationship, mom is there when daughter needs her most.

As you watch the film, consider these questions.

- In what ways are Aurora and Emma alike? How are they different?
- How does Aurora express her feelings about the choices she has made? What do you think she wishes she could go back and change?
- How does Emma feel about her mother? What does she respect about her? What does she resent?
- What advice might Aurora and Emma offer Herodias and her daughter?
- How does each woman deal with the men in their lives? What would have helped them make different choices?

- At the end, mother and daughter reach an understanding. Why does it take so long for them to recognize the strengths in the other?

One True Thing (1998) is the adaptation of a novel by Anna Quindlen. Kate (Meryl Streep) and Ellen (Renee Zellweger) are a mother and daughter who often find themselves at odds with each other. George (William Hurt) plays Kate's husband and Ellen's dad. Ellen, a rising star as a writer, goes home for her father's birthday party. There Ellen learns that her mother has cancer and she, Ellen, is expected to put her life on hold to take care of her mom. Ellen takes care of her mom and they learn more about each other than they ever dreamed.

As you watch the film, consider the following questions.

- Whose approval is Ellen seeking? How does she feel about her mother's choices? Are there parallels between the film and the biblical story? Explain your answer.

- What accounts for the conflicts between mother and daughter?

- What role does George play in the conflict and subsequent reconciliation between mother and daughter?

- What does Ellen learn about her mother and father that affects her relationship with each of them? Do you think Salome learns anything about the relationship between her mom and stepdad? What does she learn?

- What are your feelings about the ending of the film? Explain.

Postcards from the Edge (1990) is the semi-autobiographical work of Carrie Fisher. Suzanne (Meryl Streep) is a drug-addicted actress who has a love-hate relationship with her mother, Doris (Shirley MacLaine). The film chronicles Suzanne's ups and downs and her wacky relationship with her mom.

As you watch the film, consider the following questions.

- Describe the relationship between Suzanne and her mother. What are the points of conflict between them?

- How does Suzanne deal with her problems? How do you think her mother feels about her daughter's choices?

- What is the turning point in the film? How does this shape the rest of the film and Suzanne's relationship with her mother?

- If Herodias, Salome, Suzanne, and Doris were on a retreat, what might the women say to each other about how they are living their lives? What are the main lessons to be taken from the biblical story? From the film?

The Joy Luck Club (1995) is the adaptation of a novel by Amy Tan. It is a collection of stories about the lives of four immigrant Chinese mothers and their four Chinese-American daughters. The mothers go to great lengths to provide better lives for their daughters, who seem disconnected from and unappreciative of their roots. The story centers on June (Ming-Na Wen), who replaces her deceased mother at the mah-jongg games she attended regularly with her friends. The game provides the occasion for the sharing of stories of flight from Communist China and the adjustment to a different life in the United States. Through flashbacks, we get the stories and perspectives of the older women. The mostly Asian and Asian-American cast work together to share a story of hardship and triumph against the odds.

As you watch the film, consider the following questions.

- What is the significance of the mah-jongg game for the older women? Why is the gathering so important to them?

- What are the differences between the mothers and their daughters? What do the mothers hope for their daughters?

- In what ways do the daughters assert their independence? How do their strategies hurt their mothers?

- What traditions and values matter to the mothers? What values do the daughters hold? What traditions and values matter to Herodias? To her daughter?

- What are some of the generational and cultural differences between first and second generation immigrant women?

Delores Claiborne (1995) is based on a work by Stephen King. Delores (Kathy Bates) is accused of murdering her rich employer, Vera (Judy Parfitt). Delores's daughter Selena (Jennifer Jason Leigh), a news reporter in New York, returns to her small Maine hometown. Selena has tried to escape her troubled childhood, but she has made bad choices. Her tense relationship with her mother leads her on a journey of discovery and understanding.

As you watch the film, consider the following questions.

- Describe the relationship between Dolores and Vera. In what ways are the women alike? How do they differ?

- Why does Selena resent her mother? In what ways does the film illustrate the biblical story? Explain.

- Does Selena think Dolores killed her father? Does she think Dolores killed Vera?

- What options for a peaceful life does Dolores have? What advice do you think Herodias would offer Delores? What advice do you think Salome would offer Selena?

- What does Selena learn about her mother and father that changes her outlook? Do you think Selena will find happiness (if you imagine beyond the scope of the film)? Why or why not?

- Do you think Salome ever finds peace in her life after the John the Baptist incident? Explain.

7

MARY AND ELIZABETH

On the surface, the story of these two women provides a relief from the male drama of the Gospels. Both women embody power and provide a beautiful picture of women who care about each other.

Read

Luke 1:39–56

The Back Story

At the close of Malachi in the Hebrew Bible (Old Testament), the people wait for a word from God. For centuries, the people, who have been used to hearing from God, call upon a God who is silent. And the people wait. With the Gospels, the people rejoice because God opens the lines of communication again and the hope for restoration as a nation is revived. The words of Isaiah echo throughout the land—God is doing a new thing. God's new thing begins not with monarchs and power structures but rather with an elderly couple and the birth of their child.

Luke opens his Gospel with birth narratives announcing John the Baptist and Jesus of Nazareth. In these narratives, the mothers—Elizabeth and Mary—take center stage. We anticipate that something special is about to happen.

The narratives announcing the births (the annunciations) follow a set pattern:

- The appearance of an angel representing God;
- The person visited responds with fear;
- The angel delivers a special message, calling the woman by name, stating there is no need for fear, announcing the birth of a son who will do great things, giving the name of the child;
- The person visited resists the announcement;
- The angel provides a sign verifying the announcement.

Concerning John the Baptist, the annunciation is given to Zechariah, a priest of the Temple and husband of Elizabeth (see Luke 1:11–20). Note that both Zechariah and Elizabeth are righteous and obey the commands of the Torah. Zechariah is from the priestly order of Abijah and Elizabeth comes from a priestly family herself. They are a faithful couple—righteous and blameless and adherents to the Torah. The issue is that they have no children; Elizabeth is barren. Both husband and wife are getting on in years, implying that they are either past childbearing years or approaching it quickly. Suspense is being built as we remember the stories of Abraham and Sarah and Jacob and Rachel.

As Zechariah carries out his duties, he is visited by an angel. As we have seen in other narratives, the barren wife threatens to thwart God's promises. Yet, God "remembers" Elizabeth just as God "remembers" Sarah and Rachel—this implies that God, all powerful, opens the wombs of these women so that God's promises will be fulfilled. The barren Elizabeth does not enlist the help of a surrogate, as did Sarah. God remembers her and opens her womb so that she becomes pregnant (see Luke 1:24–25). The prediction about John's role is outlined—he will be filled with the Holy Spirit and bring many people to God. Not only that, he will stand in the tradition of Elijah—righting wrongs within families, turning disobedience into wisdom, and preparing people for God's Messiah. After Elizabeth conceives, she isolates herself for five months. The text does not tell us why she secludes herself—perhaps, she needs time to adjust to her new situation.

In Elizabeth's sixth month, the angel Gabriel visits a young woman in Nazareth named Mary. She is engaged to Joseph. The annunciation follows the same pattern noted, except that it is given directly to her and not to her betrothed (see Luke 1:29–38). Her child, to be named Jesus, will be greater than John—miracle of miracles! While we can assume that Zechariah and Elizabeth have been praying for a child, Mary is caught by surprise. She's not even married yet, but she is given the details of her future.

Betrothal in biblical times was a period of a year in which the bride-to-be would live in her father's house, preparing for marriage. The groom would then move her into his home and a week-long wedding celebration would follow. For all intents and purposes, the marriage becomes legal after the engagement.

Gabriel visits Mary and assures her that all things are in order because God is the architect of her future. Her child, Jesus, is destined for great things—while John prepares the way, Jesus is the Way. God's promises to David are about to be fulfilled (see Luke 1:32–33). Gabriel answers her questions and concerns. She learns that her relative, believed to be her cousin, Elizabeth, is pregnant despite being old and barren. God breaks into human history again and unfolds the divine plan. Mary consents to the annunciation and places her will within God's plan.

The Episode

After Mary consents to God's will for her, she leaves Nazareth for the hill country to visit her cousin Elizabeth. Although she is not commanded to go to Elizabeth, Mary makes haste to visit with her.

Perhaps she is motivated by joy at Elizabeth's pregnancy and wants to celebrate both of their pregnancies. The text is silent about why she moves with haste to the hill country. There is an intention to be with Elizabeth—and at her greeting, Elizabeth's baby leaps in her womb. This was no ordinary or normal movement—the baby leaps for joy! What is more, Elizabeth herself is filled with the Holy Spirit and exclaims Mary's blessedness. This is one happy re-union—the older woman, round and plump, the younger woman in the early stages of her pregnancy. Clearly both women are happy for the other and they rejoice in their good fortune.

In response to Elizabeth's exclamations, Mary breaks out in song, the now familiar Magnificat. It mirrors Hannah's song at the birth of her son, Samuel (see 1 Sam. 2:1–10). Mary identifies with the lowly and rejoices in what God is already doing in and through her. Her song moves into the political realm—the over-throw of the powerful; the scattering of the proud; the lifting up of the weak; the feeding of the hungry; the sending away empty of the rich—and depicts the reversal of what we would expect. In the midst of the oppressive and dominant powers of Rome and other rulers before, the poor, the weak, the marginalized now have renewed hope that God has not forgotten them. Now the widows, the orphans, the foreigners have reason to hope, for God is once again connecting to God's people. God is fulfilling God's promises and exercising God's power. Mary's Magnificat rejoices at God's mercy and redeeming activities.

Mary stays with Elizabeth for three months and leaves just be-fore Elizabeth delivers John. Scripture does not tell us what they did for those three months, but we can fill in some blanks. I sup-pose that they spent time in prayer and celebration. Perhaps they shared stories about their pregnancies. I imagine Mary had a lot of questions about pregnancy and childbirth. It may be that Eliz-abeth spent time teaching Mary how to care for a child, how to be a good wife, how to cook and clean. It is not clear from the text where Mary's own mother is and why Mary chooses to spend an extended time with Elizabeth. Perhaps Mary leaves Elizabeth so she can be tutored and cared for by her own mother back in Nazareth.

Elizabeth and Mary give us another example of women working together and supporting each other. Theirs is pure joy and we are caught up in their stories. Both enjoy surprises and the unexpected. Elizabeth, the older, wiser, pious woman, loves her cousin and expresses no jealousy or animosity that Mary will give birth to the Savior of the world. She is happy in her own situation and is confident that her contribution to the redemption of the world is important.

Mary, who could have gotten caught up in her own situation, wastes no time and embarks on a dangerous journey to be with her cousin. We assume that Mary has an entourage that travels with her, but we are not told whether there are men in her traveling party to provide safety. Seemingly without counting the costs, she makes up her mind and off she goes. She arrives safely and returns home safely—she is one courageous woman.

The Contemporary Connection

Here is a case of women helping women. The elder woman fully embraces the younger. Both are happy for each other and they enjoy each other's company for three months. Imagine the stories they share, the laughter they share, and the sheer joy they share. The impending birth of a child is usually the occasion for happy times. We wait in anticipation to meet the new arrival and rejoice at the birth of an addition to the family.

Women have often supported each other during pregnancy and childbirth. Older women are more than happy to share whatever knowledge they have about childbirth and care. When my mother delivered my siblings, she depended on her mother to help care for us. My grandmothers were happy to put their lives on hold to help my mother—they cooked, cleaned, and took care of the rest of us so that my mother could focus on the newborn. Having a baby is a family affair—everyone wants to be involved.

Throughout the ages, women share a special bond when they give birth. What a wonderful example Elizabeth and Mary provide for us.

Food for Thought

1. What do you think Elizabeth did during her five months of seclusion? Where were her female relatives and friends? How do you suppose they supported her? How have you supported your friends who have had children?

2. Why do you think Mary dropped everything and journeyed to be with Elizabeth? Have you ever done a similar thing for a friend? Share as much as you feel comfortable.

3. If you have given birth, share what you enjoyed about being pregnant. Share any challenges you experienced.

4. In what ways do women carry the future in their bodies? How can women without children make a contribution to the future? Do you think a mother's attitude during pregnancy affects the child?

5. In what ways did your friendships with women change during your pregnancy and after the birth of your child? If you don't have children, did the birth of children of your friends change your relationship with them? In what ways?

Films and Television Shows

Fried Green Tomatoes (1991) is based on a novel by Fannie Flagg, *Fried Green Tomatoes at the Whistle Stop Café*. Set in Birmingham, Alabama, the film focuses on an unhappy housewife whose life changes through a friendship with an older woman. We meet Evelyn (Kathy Bates), a middle-aged, passive housewife, and Ninny

(Jessica Tandy), a resident of the nursing home where Evelyn and her husband Ed (Gailard Sartain) visit his relative. Over the course of several visits and through flashbacks, Ninny shares the story of Ruth (Mary-Louise Parker) and Idgie (Mary Stuart Masterson), whose lives are changed when Ruth's husband is murdered. In the course of their developing friendship, Ninny encourages Evelyn to find her voice and claim her place in the world.

As you watch the film, consider these questions.

- How do Ruth and Idgie become friends? What holds their friendship together?

- Highlight the elements of the film that remind you of the biblical story.

- Have you ever developed a friendship with a woman over a shared tragedy? Explain.

- In what ways do the women deal with racism at their restaurant, the Whistle Stop Café?

- What is ironic about Frank's death? Who killed Frank and what happened to his body?

- What is the result of the friendship between Evelyn and Ninny?

- What are the challenges facing women who want to be friends when there is a sizable age gap? How do they overcome the challenges?

- How do you think Elizabeth and Mary dealt with the challenges of their intergenerational relationship?

The Miracle Worker (1962), derived from Helen Keller's autobiography, *The Story of My Life,* is based on the real life relationship between Anne Sullivan and Helen. In the film, Helen (Patty Duke) is blind, mute, and deaf as a result of scarlet fever. Because of her inability to communicate and her violent tantrums, her family is on the verge of having her committed to an institution. Their last hope lies with the Perkins Institute, which dispatches Anne (Anne Bancroft) to help. After much turmoil and perseverance, Anne is able to break into Helen's world to teach her how to communicate.

As you watch the film, consider the following questions.

- What enables Sullivan to stay with her plan to teach Helen?
- What is the turning point of the film? How does this influence the rest of the film?
- What binds the woman and the girl together? How does Anne get Helen to communicate?
- In what ways does the film remind you of the story of Elizabeth and Mary?
- What is your communication style? How do you overcome communication challenges with your female friends?

You Again (2010) is a funny and twisted story of Marni (Kristen Bell), who learns that her brother Will (James Wolk) is about to marry her high school nemesis, Joanna (Odette Yustman). Marni feels she must stop the wedding by revealing who Joanna really is, the terror behind the sweet face and demeanor. Marni's mother, Gail (Jamie Lee Curtis), advises her to forget about the past and move on—until her own nemesis, Ramona (Sigourney Weaver), arrives and brings their troubled past into the present. This film is about bullying, competition, and forgiveness. The film offers a contrast to the biblical story and provides an opportunity to reflect on the challenges to close relationships between and among women.

As you watch the film, consider the following questions.

- What made Marni's life so difficult in high school? What was her relationship with Joanna? What advice do you think Elizabeth and Mary might offer the young women about friendship?

- What does Marni want from Joanna that she refuses to give? How does Marni handle the situation?

- What happened between Gail and Ramona? How do they deal with their situation?

- What was high school like for you? Were you ever bullied? Did you ever bully anyone? Have you moved on?

- What questions do you think Elizabeth might have for the mothers in the film? What questions might Mary have for the daughters?

- What happens to Grandma Bunny (Betty White) that affects the end of the film? What does the title of the film mean?

8

"Some" or "Certain" Women

We may be surprised to learn that the followers of Jesus included a large number of women. They were not "just" followers; they offered service and leadership as well as financial assistance.

Read

Luke 8:1–3

The Back Story

Sometimes when we read the Gospels about the life, ministry, death, and resurrection of Jesus, we think that only "the Twelve"—the named disciples whom the Gospels record as specifically called by Jesus—are part of his inner circle. When we read carefully, however, we find that there were multitudes of folks who pledged their allegiance to Jesus. Among them were a good number of women. We know that Jesus' movement drew men and women of various means. They were privy to Jesus' teachings and witnessed the miracles he performed. It is even likely that some of them taught and healed as well. Jesus' ministry was radically inclusive, especially for his day. Women freely followed him and exercised their leadership and ministry gifts. The early Christian church affirmed the gifts of women. The Apostle Paul accepted the leadership of women until Greco-Roman domination re-imposed the strict patriarchic constrictions and as Christianity became more established.[1] Among the women who followed Jesus were Mary Magdalene, Joanna, and Susanna.

We are told that these women helped the Jesus movement from their own resources—service and money, among other contributions. Some biblical commentators suggest that the women provided domestic services for Jesus and the Twelve. The word used for these kind of services offered, *diakonia*,[2] is a general term that ranges from cooking and sewing to the work of discipleship. But other scholars suggest that the women did not provide domestic services or typical "woman's work" because Jesus' ministry was so public and took place outside the home; therefore, it would not have been appropriate for the woman to serve only as domestics. And we see in the Gospels that Jesus and the Twelve are responsible for finding and providing their food, a job that would have been relegated to servant women. We find Jesus often hanging out at people's homes, enjoying warm hospitality. So we must not assume that the women who followed Jesus only did the cooking and cleaning.

The word for "resources" that Luke uses to speak of the women's contributions means "possessions, property, and/or money." Thus, we may safely conclude that these women were independent and free-thinking, and used their resources of time, talent, and treasure (inherited or earned) to hear the message of Jesus and follow him, just as the Twelve did. Despite the speculation about who these women were and how they accumulated their resources, we know only that they were women of means who chose to follow Jesus.

Whenever "some" or "certain" women are mentioned, we find Mary Magdalene, who plays an important role in the work of Jesus from its beginning to his resurrection. Isn't it interesting that she is almost always around? We might even count her as a disciple. Because she is usually named first, we can surmise that she is the leader of the group of women who follow Jesus. Mary is not mentioned in connection with a man in her life; we read of no father, brother, uncle, husband, or son. Instead, she is associated with a city, Magdala. Magdala is thought to have been situated on the west side of the Sea of Galilee and just north of Tiberius, a prominent fishing village.

All four Gospels testify to the presence of women going all the way with Jesus—to the cross, to anointing his body for burial, to the empty tomb, and to the resurrection. Some scholars see the resurrection witnesses of women as strong affirmation of the historicity of the resurrection itself. If any of the Twelve had made the claim that Jesus was raised, they may have been dismissed as seeking to save face for their failed movement. Women were not legal witnesses and their accounts in the Gospels lend credence to the testimonies.

The Episode

There are a number of women who join the Jesus movement—not simply as spectators, but also as workers and financial contributors. These women—single and married—leave their homes to support the work of Jesus. These women, identified variously as "certain" women and "some" women, risk their reputations to follow the itinerant preacher and religious reformer. It seems that a good number of these women controlled their own money and certainly made decisions for themselves. Although we are not told the specifics of their contributions, we assume that they are active participants in the movement who are able to pay their own way to be a part of the group that travels with Jesus.

In the text from Luke, we learn the names of some and a bit about their background. We learn that there were some women who had been healed of various ailments. Mary Magdalene experienced an exorcism in which "seven demons" were cast out—the number seven indicates that she was severely afflicted. Yet she was healed and, in gratitude, she followed Jesus.

Joanna is married to a servant of Herod's, which means that she and her husband may have had a conflict about her choice to follow Jesus. Her husband, Chuza, works for the very person who opposes Jesus—imagine the conversations around their dinner table! Whatever negative feelings Chuza has about Jesus are ignored as Joanna makes her choice to follow and support Jesus. There are many more women who follow Jesus, too. They are unnamed and counted as part of the close group that gathers around Jesus.

The women have found someone in whom they can believe, and so they willingly follow Jesus. They work together to support the Jesus movement. With Mary Magdalene as their leader, they travel and do what they can to be supportive of Jesus and each other. The women engage in ministry and mission—they work for something bigger than themselves. We cannot know the sacrifices they make to follow their calling. Surely, they were talked about and encountered the scorn of others who thought they should be home taking care of husbands and children.

Mary Magdalene is shown as a loyal friend and follower of Jesus. In all four of the Gospels, she is listed among those (including women) who witness Jesus' ministry, death, and resurrection. In fact, she is instructed to tell the others (including the Twelve) about Jesus' resurrection—she is our first evangelist and preacher!

She is a consistent conversation partner with Jesus, highlighting the trust and respect that Jesus has for her. She is spiritually grounded and smart. We can assume that she is a good leader, because we don't hear about any conflicts among the women who follow Jesus. Within the frame of patriarchy, Mary Magdalene, Joanna, Susanna, and the many women who follow Jesus cannot be ignored. These women are enlightened and empowered to engage in meaningful ministry and mission despite the limitations of women during their day.

The Contemporary Connection

The work of the women in the Gospels who follow Jesus is important. They let us know that Jesus did not discriminate against women and that he welcomed their contributions to the coming reign of God. Despite the limited role for women during that time, this group of women were accepted and affirmed. Their support for the Jesus movement was welcomed and appreciated.

They can be counted as forerunners to the feminist movement of the twentieth century. They model the independent, self-sufficient, thinking women who are not afraid to chart their own course. They remind us that women have power to change the world. The adage "the hand that rocks the cradle rules the world" may be part of these women's stories.

There are examples in popular culture of women working together to bring change. Women in solidarity with each other can move mountains and bring new light to issues and concerns. In addition, women supporting women can be a powerful witness to what happens when women use their power in constructive ways.

There is much to be done to make our world safe for women and all people. When women exercise their power, they can make a difference in both small and huge ways. The task of mobilizing women can be challenging—women (and men) want to know that their efforts mean something. Women certainly share some concerns, especially regarding their children and families and in the workplace. Church and society are richer when women collectively lend their time, talent, and treasure to worthy causes and issues.

Food for Thought

1. What do you think makes Mary Magdalene a good leader? What qualities does she exhibit that make other women follow her?

2. Have you ever given leadership to a cause or on behalf of a concern? What was the reason for your leadership?

3. What role does mentoring have in leadership development and support? Have you ever been mentored? Have you ever mentored someone? Describe the relationships and their outcomes.

4. There has been great speculation about the seven demons that afflicted Mary Magdalene. Some suggested include depression, fear, bitterness, and low self-esteem, among others. What "demons" do you struggle with? How do your friends help you cope with and overcome these issues and concerns?

5. Name a cause championed by women that you support. What cause that affects women, either locally or globally, would you like to see addressed? What are you willing to contribute to such a cause?

Films and Television Shows

The Secret Life of Bees (2008), based on the novel by Sue Monk Kidd and adapted for the screen by Gina Prince-Bythewood, is a film that takes place in South Carolina during 1964. Fourteen-year-old Lily Owens (Dakota Fanning) has lost her mother, who has died. With her caregiver and friend Rosaleen (Jennifer Hudson), Lily leaves her abusive father. They end up in another town, where they are taken in by the bee-keeping Boatwright sisters, who are fiercely independent and wise: August (Queen Latifah), June (Alicia Keys), and May (Sophie Okonedo). The women care for Lily and help her learn more about her mother. The women provide a safe and loving home for Lily as she discovers who she is.

As you watch the film, consider the following questions.

- Why does Lily think she killed her mother? What items of her mother's does Lily keep hidden?

- What values does the biblical story point to? Which of these are found in the film?

- What is missing in Lily's life? How do the Boatwright sisters help her find answers?

- In what ways does the film underscore the importance of hope? What do the bees symbolize? Are there parallels to the biblical story of the women? Name and explain the connections.
- What is the significance of the sisters' names?
- In what ways are the sisters like a mother to Lily? What does Lily learn about love and family from the sisters?

The Women of Brewster Place (1984) is a two-part miniseries based on the novel by Gloria Naylor. The film revolves around the lives of a group of strong women who live in a depressed neighborhood. The major characters are Mattie Michael (Oprah Winfrey), Etta Mae (Jackée Harry), Kiswana (Robin Givens), Theresa (Paula Kelly), Ciel (Lynn Whitfield), Lorraine (Lonette McKee), and Cora Lee (Phyllis Yvonne Stickney). They struggle to overcome relationships with abusive men, sorrow, poverty, racism, and dysfunctional family issues. They find solid friendship and support among the other women who live on Brewster Place.

As you watch the film, consider the following questions.

- Describe the friendship between Mattie and Etta Mae. What connects the women? How do they deal with their different worldviews and desires?
- What kind of relationship does Mattie have with Ciel? What do they learn about themselves and each other through their friendship?
- In what ways do the women of Brewster Place go against the norm, as do the biblical women?
- Kiswana fights for change and wants to see it happen quickly. What causes tension with her mother (Cicely Tyson)? How does Mrs. Browne see her role as mother?
- What is the turning point in the film? How does the turning point shape the ending of the film?

- What is the significance of the wall? How does the wall bring the women together?
- The biblical women are pioneers in that they are powerful leaders in the early days of Christianity. How are the women of Brewster Place pioneers?

Mona Lisa Smile (2003) is a film about an art professor who wants to expand the choices for her young college students in the 1950s. Katherine (Julia Roberts) leaves her boyfriend in Los Angeles and takes a teaching position at Wellesley College, a private women's college in Massachusetts. Her students are smart and seem to have it all together. She challenges her students to think outside the box and meets resistance because many of them are preparing to be wives and mothers rather than career women. One student, Betty (Kirsten Dunst), challenges Katherine and the more liberal members of her class. Betty intends to marry and is not interested in feminism. The film is about the challenges presented by the emerging women's movement and one professor's attempt to widen the horizons for her students.

As you watch the film, consider the following questions.

- How does Katherine develop her "liberal" views? How do her views differ from the culture at Wellesley?
- The biblical women "see" something that the wider community does not. What does Katherine "see" that her students do not?
- Why do Katherine and Betty clash? What issue is at the heart of their disagreement? In what ways are they similar?
- Can women "have it all"—a balance among career, marriage, and children? Why or why not? Do you think the biblical women had it all? Explain.
- How does Katherine deal with her frustration? How do you deal with frustration?

- Can women with vastly different worldviews become friends? Why or why not?

Desperate Housewives (2004–2012) is a series about the women who live on Wisteria Lane, their trials, tribulations, and troubled friendships with each other. The show is narrated by a deceased neighbor, Mary Alice Young (Brenda Strong), who committed suicide. Behind closed doors, the women deal with various domestic and family problems and keep secrets while trying to maintain a perfect suburban life. The ensemble cast includes Felicity Huffman as Lynette Scavo, Teri Hatcher as Susan Mayer , Marcia Cross as Bree Van de Kamp, and Eva Longoria as Gabrielle Solis. Each season brings new dilemmas, crimes, secrets, and cast members. While there is no clear "leader" among the women, each exercises leadership in the various situations depicted on the show.

As you watch the show, consider the following questions.

- Describe the relationships among the women. What characterizes their friendships?

- In what ways do the women rely on and trust each other? Why do they keep secrets from each other?

- In what ways does the show mirror the values and challenges of the women in the biblical text?

- Which of the women on the show would you like as a friend? Why?

- Describe each woman's personality. In what ways are the women similar? In what ways are they different?

- What advice might Mary Magdalene offer the women of Wisteria Lane?

9

MARTHA AND MARY

Martha and Mary are sisters who squabble over household duties. They are close despite their differences. The two seem to be polar opposites, but we find that they are very much alike.

Read

Luke 10:38–42

The Back Story

The story of Martha, Mary, and Lazarus is a familiar one. They live in Bethany, about two miles from Jerusalem. Although we don't know how Jesus comes to know them, we find Jesus at their home on a couple of occasions. Jesus enjoys their hospitality and seems very comfortable in their presence. We don't know many details about the siblings; we don't know who their parents are or how the three come to live together under the same roof.

In the Gospel According to John, we meet Martha and Mary again (see John 11:1–45). In John 11, Martha and Mary send word to Jesus that their brother Lazarus is ill. Jesus doesn't respond immediately to their request for a visit to heal Lazarus. In fact, Jesus waits four days before heading to Bethany. He is met by Martha, who leaves the mourners to meet him on the road. She dispenses with the niceties and lashes out at him (see John 11:21). If only Jesus had come when she sent word, her brother would still be alive. She isn't quite ready to give up hope that Lazarus might yet live. Jesus consoles her and says she will see Lazarus again. They launch into a theological conversation about resurrection; she believes she and her brother will be reunited at the general resurrection of the dead. According to her belief, resurrection is to be a community event of transformation (see Isa. 26:19). Jesus corrects her by stating, "I am the resurrection and the life"—the resurrection and eternal life are manifested in Jesus. In this moment, Martha receives the revelation that Jesus is God's Messiah and she confesses her faith in him. Her confession resembles that of Peter's in Matthew 16:15–16. The Gospels provide the story of a woman's confession that parallels that of one of the Twelve. She is more than capable of engaging Jesus in theological discourse. This exchange affirms that she is a leader within the circle of those who follow Jesus. And she can't wait to tell the others back at the house. She runs home and tells Mary that Jesus has arrived.

Mary runs out to meet him. She kneels before Jesus before she, too, lashes out at him for delaying his visit (John 11:32). She weeps along with her friends who have followed her out to the road to meet Jesus. Jesus adds his own weeping to the mourning before he acts. As his last public act of ministry, Jesus raises Lazarus from death.

Martha and Mary provide a portrait of earnest disciples of Jesus—active doers and hearers of the Word. The women are among Jesus' conversation partners and understand the multifaceted nature of leadership and hospitality.

The Episode

During one of his visits (in Luke's Gospel), Martha is busy making sure the guests are comfortable. Mary, on the other hand, is sitting at the feet of Jesus taking in his teachings. Mary occupies the space traditionally reserved for male rabbinical students. No one seems concerned that she is soaking up the words of Jesus. We know that those who followed Jesus included a good number of women, so her attention to Jesus does not seem to be out of the ordinary. That is, until Martha pipes in. Martha doesn't speak to her sister; instead she goes straight to Jesus with her complaint. She seems to expect Jesus to fix the situation so that Martha is not the only one taking care of the guests. But Jesus doesn't tell Mary to get up and get busy. Rather, he chastises Martha for fretting about the small things.

Commentators polarize the sisters and place them in tension with each other—Martha is too concerned with household chores. Mary is the "smart, wise" one who uses the opportunity to deepen her understanding of the faith. Martha is the one who takes care of practical needs while Mary is the contemplative, thoughtful one. Together, they form a picture of what it means to be a disciple of Jesus.

This episode comes right after the parable about the Good Samaritan (Luke 10:25–37) and just before Jesus' teaching on prayer (Luke 11:1–4). Is Luke making a statement about right discipleship? The Good Samaritan is about one who takes the time to render concrete and practical assistance to a person in distress. The Good Samaritan does not let cultural or religious barriers keep him from doing the right thing for the right reason. The help given is just what is needed. Martha's service is just what is needed. Her activity is described as *diakonia*, a Greek word that includes ministry and service as an act of faith. It is the same word that describes the work and service of the Twelve. Scholars indicate that Martha is a believer who offers table service and ministry as part of her leadership. She is active and pays attention to all the details that make her home warm and inviting. Martha is like the Good Samaritan, offering practical hospitality.

Mary is a student more concerned with listening than working. She represents the disciple who is focused on prayer and meditation. Ever the student, she is predisposed to sitting and listening and learning. She has chosen the "better" part. Jesus seems to be devaluing Martha's work in favor of Mary's.

Scholars are raising questions about whether the text is posing an either/or proposition. Is one way better than the other? Must we only choose between being active or being passive? Some suggest that there is a conflict in Luke's community (which existed after the resurrection of Jesus) over women's leadership. There was a move back to a more patriarchic way in opposition to Jesus' egalitarian stance. If this is the case, then the Gospel writer would want to silence Martha and praise Mary. However, there may be another way of viewing the text.

What if Jesus poses to Martha (and to us) that we always must make the choice? The path of discipleship will be different for each of us. Some of us are Type A's and have to be busy with our hands and feet. Others of us are Type B's and have to think things through before we act. Because this episode of the sisters is placed between the parable of the Good Samaritan and Jesus' teaching about prayer, this episode with the sisters leads us to think that Martha and Mary may be a bridge between doing and hearing the Word. If this is the case, then there is no one way to be a disciple.

Jesus does not tell Mary to leave the circle and help Martha. Jesus addresses Martha with a pastoral word and tells her that she can choose what to do. If we think Martha is a leader, we can assume that she, too, has sat at Jesus' feet to listen and learn. At some point, though, Martha decides that some things must get done. Jesus seems concerned that she is too worked up about her work— Jesus basically tells her to calm down, chill out, and decide what is more important in that moment. And the choice is always hers!

She is not locked into tradition or convention; she can, at any point, sit down, take a breath, and listen. Jesus refuses to tell her what to do but lays before her the choices.

The Contemporary Connection

The sisters illustrate that women born and raised in the same family can have very different ways of being in the world. We don't see Martha and Mary substantially interacting with each other. Except when Martha tells Mary that Jesus is asking for her when he visits them in Bethany after Lazarus died, there is no conversation between the two highlighted in the biblical text. Jesus is the mediator between the two. We know them to be smart women who are clear about what they believe. They fully engage Jesus and feel comfortable in chastising him.

We don't have information about their parents. And Lazarus does not speak; only his sisters do. We can safely assume that they are strong women who speak up for themselves and don't back down, not even with Jesus.

Sisters are sometimes in conflict with each other over a variety of issues. Birth order may play a role in how sisters interact with each other. My own sisters would probably say that I am the bossy one, almost rebellious in the ways that I interacted with our parents. My middle sister is the one who actively works to hold all the siblings together since our parents' deaths. We most often gather at her home and she makes sure we all know what we should be doing. My youngest sister works at declaring and holding on to her independence. It's so easy for my middle sister and me to tell our youngest sister what to do—but she resists and we respect her for that.

Sisters can share a special bond—they live through the same family history even though they don't always understand the dynamics to be the same. In popular culture, we find a range of sister relationships. The key is to let each woman be who she is and not try to change her. That is, we can learn to love unconditionally and support one another wholeheartedly. It is important to intervene when a sister is on the verge of hurting herself or making a really bad decision. But even under those circumstances, ultimately she is responsible for her own choices and decisions.

Food for Thought

1. Describe your relationship with your sister(s). What are sources of tension? How do you work to overcome the tensions?

2. How does your relationship with your sister(s) parallel or contrast with that between Martha and Mary?

3. Do you consider your sister also to be a friend? In what ways she is a friend? How do you distinguish between being a sibling and being a friend? Do you think Martha and Mary were also friends? Why or why not?

4. Have you ever found yourself in a competitive stance with your sister? Over what were you competitive? Has the situation been resolved? How? Or, if not, why not?

5. We have heard the expression that friends are as close as sisters. What does this mean?

6. In what ways can women support each other and, at the same time, allow each the space to make her own decisions and choices?

Films and Television Programs

Having Our Say: The Delany Sisters' First Hundred Years (1999), a film biography, is based on the lives of two extraordinary women, Sadie (Diahann Carroll) and Annie Elizabeth "Bessie" (Ruby Dee). Born in North Carolina, they are the daughters of the first African American Episcopal bishop and a biracial mother. They live through racism and sexism to achieve great success. Sadie was the first African American woman to teach domestic science in the public schools of New York. Bessie became the second African American dentist in New York. They told their remarkable story to *New York Times* reporter Amy Hill Hearth (Amy Madigan) when they were 103 and 101.

As you watch the film, consider the following questions.

- Describe the Delany sisters' childhood. What were moments of joy? What challenges did they face?

- Describe the sisters' relationship. What are points of tension? How does their relationship mirror or contrast with that of Martha and Mary?

- How do the sisters express their love and support for one another?

- Bessie declares, "Sadie is molasses. I'm vinegar." What does she mean by this? In the biblical text, which sister is molasses and which is vinegar?

- Both sisters live to be 100 plus. Do you think they have any regrets about their choices and decisions?

- The sisters believe that life is short and it is up to each of us to make it sweet. In what ways were their lives sweet? In what ways is your life sweet?

- Are there things you still want to do or accomplish? When will you start doing those things? What challenges do you anticipate along the way?

What Ever Happened to Baby Jane? (1962; for a fun video, visit http ://www.imdb.com/video/screenplay/vi836895001/) is a cult classic about sibling rivalry, starring two movie veterans, Bette Davis as Jane and Joan Crawford as Blanche. The sisters live in a mansion that has seen better days. Jane is a former child star who has never quite grown up. Her sister is a former movie star who is paralyzed and dependent on Jane for her care. Blanche spends her days watching old movies on television while Jane finds new ways to torture her sister. Jane's attempts to stage a comeback are ridiculously funny and tragically sad; she takes her anger out on her sister. After some twists and turns, the two sisters are at the beach; it is clear that Jane is losing all grip on reality. Still, the sisters have a revealing conversation as the movie winds to an end.

As you watch the film, consider the following questions.

- Describe the highlights of each sister's childhood. What is ironic about their current relationship?

- Are there ways to raise healthy children in a show business environment?

- Why is Jane guilt-ridden and angry? Is Jane more like Martha or more like Mary?

- At the beach, Jane says to her sister, "All this time, we could have been friends . . ." What does she mean by this? Do you think Martha and Mary were friends? Why or why not?

- How do you feel about the end of the film? Explain.

All about Eve (1950) is based on a short story by Mary Orr, "The Wisdom of Eve." The setting is New York and the theater world. Margo (Bette Davis) is a Broadway star who is showing her age. Her best friend Karen (Celeste Holm) is married to brilliant playwright Lloyd (Hugh Marlowe), who has the perfect play in mind for Margo. Margo's boyfriend, Bill (Gary Merrill), is younger than she is and loves her unconditionally. Enter a young, ambitious fan, Eve (Anne Baxter), who shakes up Margo's world and threatens to destroy the very lives Eve claims to respect and admire. The three women are a study in aging, mentoring, friendship, betrayal, and ambition. The film is marked by brilliant dialogue and ironic plot twists. The film is not about sisters but is about older and younger women, mentoring, and competition, which mirrors Martha and Mary's situation.

As you watch the film, consider the following questions.

- What keeps Margo grounded in the midst of stardom and fan adulation? What do you think keeps Martha grounded? What keeps Mary grounded?

- What hints are there that Eve is not the naïve wide-eyed fan she pretends to be? What secret is she keeping? How does her secret come back to haunt her?

- Margo remarks, "Fasten your seatbelts. It's going to be a bumpy ride." What does she mean by this statement?

- There is a poignant scene between Margo and Karen where Margo comments about getting older. What lessons has she learned over the course of her life and career? How do these lessons shape her future decisions?

- What advice might Martha offer Margo about choices?

- In what ways does Eve achieve her goals? Does she find what she is looking for? Do you think Martha and Mary find what each is searching for in life? Explain.

- What is ironic (and a bit scary) about the closing scene of the film?

10

L O I S   A N D   E U N I C E

We find that a grandmother and mother are responsible for passing along family traditions and values, including religious teachings, to Timothy.

Read

2 Timothy 1:5–7

The Back Story

The majority of the New Testament (also called the Continuing Testament) is in the form of letters or epistles. They deal with the work and ministry of the Apostle Paul and the organization and leadership of early Christian churches and communities. Scholars generally agree that the epistles fall into two categories: the Pauline Epistles (believed to be written by Paul and including Romans through Philemon) and the General or Pastoral Epistles (believed to be written by someone other than Paul and including Hebrews through Jude). The epistles cover a broad range of topics: theological teachings, pastoral care, teachings on lifestyle and morality, religious doctrine, religious leadership, and guidelines for community life. The epistles remind us that there was much confusion and issues that early church leaders had to handle. There were spiritual, theological, and practical issues that required attention and solutions.

One of the "problems" with the epistles is that we don't have the accompanying correspondence that would allow us a fuller picture of what is being addressed. That is, we only have half of the conversation. Scholars use external sources to help them piece together what is going on with these Christian communities and churches. It is clear from the epistles that people had some real concerns about how they should order church and life in the midst of the vast diversity of the Greek and Roman worlds in which they found themselves. Paul, as missionary and church planter, had the task of answering questions and putting out fires among the people he served. His own roots are in Judaism yet he brings an openness that embraces Gentiles, especially the poor people in ancient urban settings. Paul works in the midst of Roman dominance and oppression, with the teachings of the Torah forming the core of his message.

The General Epistles are more personal and social. Those persons being addressed are under fire because of their faith. The epistles serve to encourage them to stand strong in the face of fierce and potentially violent opposition from the powers that dominate them as well as those who pose alternative teachings and worldviews. The bottom line is that believers are to hold on to their faith and hope in the power of Jesus Christ.

We meet Timothy in Acts 16:1–5. The Apostle Paul travels to Derbe and Lystra, ancient towns near Galatia and Cappadocia, where he has many disciples. One disciple is Timothy, who is the product of a "mixed" marriage. His mother is a Jewish believer and his father is Greek. Timothy's heritage highlights the diversity of Paul's missionary team, which was held in suspicion. There were questions about how much "Jewishness" one had to have in order to be accepted in the Christian community. Paul's preaching of salvation through the grace of God was good for many; but there were believers who felt that one had to be Jewish before becoming Christian. Paul tries to strike a happy medium so that everyone will listen to his teachings.

Timothy is held in high esteem among the people in Lystra and Iconium. It is likely that he learned about the faith through the teachings of his grandmother and mother. It is noted that his mother is a believer—and we may assume that she learned the faith from her own mother. The women are the transmitters of the faith, and they have taught Timothy well.[1] There is no indication that Timothy's father hindered his son's religious development, but the implication among the people is that Timothy is not a full-fledged believer although he is learned and earnest. He is so sincere and passionate for Christ that Paul invites Timothy to accompany him on his travels and join in his work. Further, we learn that Timothy must be circumcised in order to preach and teach among the Jewish Christians (see Acts 16:3); he is now a full-fledged believer. The circumcision is not a condition of salvation, but rather an accommodation to those who might have questions about it. Paul is willing to make this concession to keep the peace between the Jews and Gentiles who populate the early churches. Timothy speaks "both-and" language by understanding what it means to be both Jewish *and* Greek—the very characteristic Paul seeks in his churches. Timothy eventually becomes an influential leader in the Christian movement.

The Episode

In 2 Timothy, we eavesdrop on Paul's instructions to the young disciple. In Paul's greeting, he emphasizes the place of prayer in his life and ministry. He implies a close relationship with Timothy that is undergirded by genuine emotion.

Paul points out the faith of Lois and Eunice, which has been passed on to Timothy. He pays homage to the women responsible for Timothy's character as well as his belief in Jesus Christ. If Timothy's faith is sincere, it is because of the sincere faith Timothy's grandmother and mother have and have in turn taught him. And because of his deep and strong faith, Paul reminds Timothy to keep the flames of faith burning hot. Timothy's gifts are not to be taken for granted but rather should spur him to even greater service.

Lois and Eunice stand in the tradition of Mary Magdalene, Martha, and Mary—they exhibit strong, deep, genuine, sincere faith that allows the believer to live in integrity and singleness of mind and spirit. We don't know how Timothy's grandmother Lois came to believe. Although Timothy's mother Eunice married a Greek, she is a believer. It may be that she was a believer before her marriage and her husband did not hinder her faith. At any rate, Paul recognizes that these two women have been instrumental in making Timothy the man he is. They make sure Timothy knows his roots, and he is convinced that a life of ministry and service is the life for him. He is a reflection of the two women. Their instructions have made Timothy a fitting missionary and colleague for Paul.

Although Timothy is schooled in his Jewish roots, he is not a practitioner of Jewish rituals. He is not circumcised. This may be due to his Greek father, who would not have seen circumcision as important or as a sign of faithfulness. His father was not Jewish and he was not Christian. Timothy assents to circumcision and leaves home for the missionary field.

The Contemporary Connection

In many homes today, the women are the ones who teach children right from wrong as well as lessons about religion and faith. During my junior high school years, I spent my summers in Birmingham, Alabama, with my maternal grandmother. My grandmother's second husband was a deacon in a Baptist church. Every Sunday morning, we studied the Sunday school lesson before breakfast. We read the scripture from the Bible and the lesson from the Sunday school book. The conversations were informative and quite interesting. We often spent the greater part of the day at church: Sunday school, worship, a break for lunch, afternoon worship, and, while the adults studied together, the young people participated in the Baptist Youth Training Union. When we returned home on Sunday evening, we would talk about the day over pound cake—sharing what we had learned and lifting up any questions that arose for us. I often had questions, and my grandmother and I would sit at the kitchen table for hours talking.

My grandmother was quite the theologian, and I learned a lot at her kitchen table. We read the Bible together and she helped me understand the essence of the texts. Her perspective on the Bible and life was grounded in her experience as a black woman who worked as a domestic in the segregated South. Her sometimes bitter experiences of racism and sexism, however, were tempered by a deep faith that she was a child of God. She knew that how she earned money did not define her, her faith did. My grandmother, proud and strong, did not let the circumstances of life get her down—she always maintained hope that a better day was on the way. She made it clear, though, that while there was a brighter day coming, that did not stop her from doing whatever she could to make this life better. She told stories of her own resistance to racism in Alabama and encouraged me to find ways to make a better life for myself and for all blacks. At her kitchen table, I learned about being black, being a woman, and being concerned and active on behalf of others.

My mother also instilled Christian values in her children. I remember walking with my mother in the snow to a church near our home in Chicago. The weather didn't matter—we walked to the neighborhood church. When my brother was born, my mother did not want to take him out in the wintry elements, but she made sure that I got to church. She asked neighbors to let me accompany them. It was important to her that I got to church, even when she couldn't make it.

My faith is shaped by the early examples of my grandmother and mother. They answered my early questions about Christianity. As I got older, we engaged in lively conversations about how to apply Christian values to everyday life and life's dilemmas. I owe my foundation in the faith to these strong women. Perhaps this is your story, too.

Food for Thought

1. Who laid the foundation of faith for you? In what ways was the faith instilled in you?

2. How do you imagine Lois learned the faith? In what ways might Lois and Eunice have transmitted the faith to Timothy?

3. To whom do you address questions about religion that you may have? Are you satisfied with answers you've received to your questions?

4. If you have children, how do you decide what to teach them? How does your church help transmit the faith to your children?

5. What do you need as an adult to continue learning about faith and values?

Films and Television Shows

Soul Food (1997) is the story of a Chicago family, the Josephs, that gathers every Sunday for a soul food dinner. While the food is incredibly delicious, it serves as the setting for sharing stories about the old days and the passing on of family traditions and values. When matriarch Mama Jo (Irma B. Hall) becomes increasingly ill, her family begins to unravel. The story of the Joseph family, told through the eyes of eleven-year-old Ahmed, is one of tensions that lie just below the surface. The three sisters seem incapable of holding the family together. The eldest, Teri (Vanessa L. Williams), is rich and successful except when it comes to love and marriage. Her current husband, Miles (Michael Beach), is a successful attorney whose life's ambition is to be a musician. Teri is always on edge because the family looks to her whenever there is a financial crisis. The middle sister, Maxine (Vivica A. Fox), appears to be the most stable of the family with a strong marriage and sweet children. Her husband, Kenny (Jeffrey Sams), dated Teri for a while but dropped her for Maxine. Maxine feels that Teri does not respect family traditions and uses her money to bully other family members. The youngest sister, Bird (Nia Long), surprises the family by marrying Lem, a former inmate. When Lem (Meki Phifer) loses his job, Bird turns to a former boyfriend to get her husband a job. Of course, her intentions are misinterpreted and lead to troubles in her marriage.

As each sister gets caught up in her own drama and in the drama with each other, Ahmed (Brandon Hammond) is left with the task of finding ways to keep the family together.

As you watch the film, consider the following questions.

- Mama Jo is the glue that holds the family together. What are some of the values she passes down to her children?

- In what ways does Mama Jo's spiritual leadership in the home mirror that of Lois and Eunice?

- In what ways does each of the sisters embody the Joseph family values? How do they defy or resist them? How do you compare the daughters' spirituality to Timothy's?

- Why does Teri have such a difficult time with relationships? What do you think her sisters would advise her to do?

- What finally brings the family back together? Do you think they will stay connected? Why or why not?

- What traditions does your family treasure and try to pass on to future generations? How do you live out these traditions and values? What advice might Timothy offer the sisters about moving into the future?

Down in the Delta (1998) is a film directed by Maya Angelou. Living in a Chicago project, Rosa Lynn (Mary Alice) tries to save her family and pass along important family values. Her daughter, Loretta (Alfre Woodard), is undereducated and addicted to drugs. She has two children and relies on her mother for support. Rosa Lynn sends Loretta and her children to stay with her brother Earl (Al Freeman Jr.) in Mississippi. There, Loretta befriends Zenia (Loretta Devine) and learns the meaning of friendship, trust, and family.

As you watch the film, consider the following questions.

- Who is "Nathan"? Why is he important to the plot?

- Describe the relationship between Rosa Lynn and Loretta. What are the challenges in their relationship?

- How do Loretta and Zenia become friends? What do they learn from each other?

- How do you feel about the ending of the film? What would you change?

- What are some values that Rosa Lynn wants her family to learn and cherish? How does her daughter embody those values? Would you say Loretta is more like or different from Timothy? Explain.

Beloved (1998) is based on Toni Morrison's novel. The story takes place shortly after the Civil War with flashbacks to earlier times. The focus is on Sethe (Orpah Winfrey), who lives near Cincinnati and is a former slave. Her life's trials, tribulations, and triumphs form the basis for the plot. She shares her story with her daughters, Denver (Kimberly Elise) and Beloved (Thandie Newton). The film delves into the brutality of slavery, the unwavering spirituality that helped the slaves to survive, and the role of family and friendship in the midst of trying circumstances.

As you watch the film, consider the following questions.

- What secrets does Sethe harbor? How are those secrets affecting her life? How do Sethe's secrets affect Denver's life?

- What is the significance of Beloved's name?

- In what ways is spirituality portrayed in the film? Who is the main transmitter of faith and spirituality? How does the transmission of faith in the film mirror that in Timothy's story?

- Describe the relationship between Sethe, Denver, and Beloved. What does each get from the relationship?

- What role do the neighbor church women play when they visit Sethe's home?

- What lessons do you take away from the film? From the biblical text?

Steel Magnolias (1989) is a film that highlights the relationship among a group of women in Shreveport, Louisiana. The characters are strong and weather a number of ups and downs. They include Truvy (Dolly Parton), who owns a beauty shop; Annelle (Daryl Hannah), a recent beauty school graduate; M'Lynn (Sally Field), friend of Truvy's, who is getting married; Shelby (Julia Roberts), M'Lynn's daughter, who has diabetes; and a group of women who hang out at the beauty shop, including the negative widow Ouiser (Shirley MacLaine) and the happy-go-lucky widow Clairee (Olympia Dukakis). Shelby's high-risk pregnancy creates angst and tension for the women, especially her mother. The intergenerational nature of the film connects us to the story of Lois and Eunice in passing along values and lessons to the next generation.

As you watch the film, consider the following questions.

- What draws the eclectic group of women together? What holds their friendships together?
- Describe the relationship between M'Lynn and Shelby. In what ways is their relationship healthy? In what ways is it unhealthy?
- How do M'Lynn's friends support her? How do they challenge her?
- What challenges do you imagine Lois and Eunice encountered around their teachings for Timothy?
- What challenges have you faced in transmitting values and traditions to your children or grandchildren?
- In what ways are the women like steel? In what ways are they like magnolias? Do you think Lois and Eunice consider themselves to be steel and/or magnolias? Explain.

A CLOSING WORD

In *Girlfriends: Exploring Women's Relationships in the Bible*, we have had the opportunity to look at ten biblical stories that help us see women in relationship with each other. The stories are woman-focused and teach us lessons about who we are, individually and in relationship to and with others. In addition, we have had the opportunity to look at elements of our culture that connect us to the biblical stories.

Some of the stories leave us with positive lessons:

- Shiphrah and Puah show what happens when women use their power for good instead of evil;
- Jephthah's daughter and her friends teach us lessons about living and dying, and that death is not the end to friendship;
- Ruth and Naomi teach us that age is no barrier to meaningful friendships and that family ties are not based solely on blood ties;
- Elizabeth and Mary teach us about the joy of being with a good friend who listens and shares in our joys;
- "Some" or "certain" women teach us that women who rally around a common goal or passion can exercise power and leadership that can change the world;
- Lois and Eunice show us the importance of transmitting values and traditions to our children so they may grow up grounded and rooted in things that matter.

Of course, not all the stories leave us with positive lessons; some teach us what *not* to do:

- Sarah and Hagar show us that ultimately barriers of race and class are artificial and keep us from genuinely connecting with other women;

- Leah and Rachel show us the kind of conflict and scheming that results when we see other women as competitors rather than allies;

- Herodias and her daughter show us what happens when we let our emotions dictate our choice and decisions—sometimes the outcome is good; other times, it is tragic. They also show us the importance of passing along positive and life-giving values.

- Martha and Mary show us that we are often different sides of the same coin rather than enemies.

These stories—biblical and contemporary—help us to see what can happen when we women risk connecting with other women. Women united can accomplish more than we can as individuals. I hope these studies are just the beginning of connecting the Bible with real life. I encourage you to continue studying the Bible to see how our lives parallel and mirror the stories we encounter in scripture.

Further, I hope these stories help us to value our friendships with other women. When push comes to shove, our friends will be there to lend a helping hand. Do not underestimate the value and joy of having friends who love and support you. Even though I spend a lot of time alone, preparing sermons and writing books, I rely on my friends, my girlfriends, to keep me grounded and sane. My girlfriends make me laugh and they take me out of my world. They invite me to participate in their lives and the lives of their children. They remind me that I am not alone in this world.

They make me know that I can count on them, in good times and in challenging ones.

Some of my girlfriends have passed on and I miss them dearly. Whenever I get sad, though, I can hear one or the other telling me to "buck up and move on." They are not encouraging me to forget them; rather, they are telling me to rejoice that we had time together and not to miss opportunities to connect with and enjoy others.

Some of my most rewarding and most difficult relationships have been with women. And I don't regret any moments I've shared with my friends. Please take the time to nurture and deepen your ties with your women friends. May we forgive the women who have betrayed or shunned us; and may we be forgiven for those negative acts we have done to other women.

The bottom line is that we need each other—may these stories help us to offer grace and love toward each other and to ourselves.

NOTES

INTRODUCTION

1. OMG—"Oh my Gosh/God!"; BTW—"By the way"; BRB—"Be right back"; ROFL—"Rolling on the floor laughing"; LOL—"laughing out loud." ☺

2. Ellen Michaud, "Women, Stress, and Friendship," http://www .support4change.com/index.php?option=com_content&view=article&id= 129:women-stress-and-friendship&catid=44:friends&Itemid=175, accessed 10/19/10; from Ellen Michaud, "Your Secret Weapon against Stress," *Prevention Magazine* (August, 2001), 130–37.

3. Ellen Goodman and Gail O'Brien, *I Know Just What You Mean: The Power of Friendship in Women's Lives* (New York: Touchstone, 2000), 11–66.

4. Gale Berkowitz, "UCLA Study on Friendship among Women: An Alternative to Fight or Flight," 2002, http://www.anapsid.org/cnd/gender /tendfend.html, accessed 6/30/2010.

CHAPTER ONE

1. For instance, see Rebekah (Gen. 25:19–21), Rachel (Gen. 30), and Hannah (1 Sam. 1).

CHAPTER THREE

1. Two other instances where we find women who obey God at the risk of defying human rulers are in 2 Samuel 21:1–13, where Rizpah defies King David by watching over the bodies of her slain family, and 2 Kings 22:11–20, where Huldah the prophet risks death by giving King Josiah the truth about God's plan for Israel.

CHAPTER FOUR

1. Othniel, Ehud, Shamgar, Deborah, Gideon/Abimelech, Tola, Jair, Jephthah, Ibzan, Elon, Abdon, and Samson; see Judges 3–13.

CHAPTER EIGHT

1. For further study, see Elisabeth Schüssler Fiorenza, *In Memory of Her: A Feminist Theological Reconstruction of Christian Origins* (New York: Crossroad/Herder & Herder, 1994); Barbara E. Reid, *Choosing the Better Part? Women in the Gospel of Luke* (Collegeville, MN: Liturgical Press, 1996); Bonnie Thurston, *Women in the New Testament: Questions and Commentary* (New York: Crossroad, 1998); Frances Taylor Gench, *Back to the Well:*

Women's Encounter with Jesus in the Gospels (Louisville: Westminster John Knox Press, 2004).

2. H. W. Beyer, *"diakoné, diakonía, diákonos,"* *Theological Dictionary of the New Testament,* edited by Gerhard Kittel and Gerhard Friedrich, trans. by Geoffrey W. Bromiley (Grand Rapids, MI: William B. Eerdmans, 1985), 152–55.

CHAPTER 10

1. There are other biblical women who exercise spiritual leadership, notably Deborah (Judges 5), Samson's mother (Judges 13), Hannah (1 Samuel 1), and Huldah (2 Kings 8).

RESOURCES FOR FURTHER STUDY

BOOKS

Apter, Terri, and Ruthellen Josselson. *Best Friends: The Pleasures and Perils of Girls' and Women's Friendships.* New York: Three Rivers Press, 1998.

Chittister, Joan. *The Friendship of Women: The Hidden Tradition of the Bible.* New York: Blue Bridge, 2006.

Essex, Barbara J. *Bad Girls of the Bible: Exploring Women of Questionable Virtue* Cleveland: United Church Press, 1999.

————. *More Bad Girls of the Bible* Cleveland: Pilgrim Press, 2009.

————. *Women in the Bible: Insights Bible Studies for Growing.* Cleveland: Pilgrim Press, 2001.

Gilkes, Cheryl Townsend. *"If It Wasn't for the Women . . ." Black Women's Experience and Womanist Culture in Church and Community.* Maryknoll, NY: Orbis, 2001.

Goodman, Ellen, and Patricia O'Brien. *I Know Just What You Mean: The Power of Friendships in Women's Lives.* New York: Simon & Schuster, 2000.

Levine, Irene S. *Best Friends Forever: Surviving a Breakup with Your Best Friend.* New York: Overlook TP, 2009.

Pipher, Mary. *Reviving Ophelia: Saving the Selves of Adolescent Girls.* New York: Ballantine Books, 1995.

Pryor, Liz. *What Did I Do Wrong? When Women Don't Tell Each Other the Friendship Is Over.* New York: Free Press, 2009.

Rind, Patricia. *Women's Best Friends: Beyond Betty, Veronica, Thelma, and Louise.* New York: Haworth Press, 2002.

Rubin, Lillian. *Just Friends: The Role of Friendship in Our Lives.* New York: Harper, 1986.

Weems, Renita J. *Just A Sister Away: A Womanist Vision of Women's Relationships in the Bible.* San Diego: LuraMedia, 1988.

Winter, Miriam Therese. *WomanWisdom: A Feminist Lectionary and Psalter, Women of the Hebrew Bible Scriptures: Part One.* New York: Crossroads, 1991.

————. *WomanWitness: A Feminist Lectionary and Psalter, Women of the Hebrew Scriptures: Part Two.* New York: Crossroads, 1997.

———. *Woman Word: A Feminist Lectionary and Psalter, Women of the New Testament.* New York: Crossroads, 1990.

Zaslow, Jeffrey. *The Girls from Ames: A Story of Women and Forty-Year Friendship.* New York: Gotham Books, 2009.

DOCUMENTARIES

Best Friends: The Power of Sisterhood. American Public Television, 2006. Hosted by Jamie Lee Curtis.

WEBSITES

Confidence Coalition. http://confidencecoalition.org/nationalwomens friendshipmonth. Online community founded in 2009 by Kappa Delta Sorority; umbrella group is the Confidence Coalition, formed to mobilize organizations, companies, and individuals that promote self-esteem and confidence among girls and women. Information about and resources for International Women's Friendship Month.

Diva Girl Parties. http://www.diva-girl-parties-and-stuff.com/index.html. Find resources and celebration ideas here to commemorate friendships.

Frienship4Me Facebook page. https://www.facebook.com/friendship4me. A free online community to help women who have difficulty finding female friends, founded by Debbie and Karen, two stay-at-home moms.

Girlfriendology. http://www.girlfriendology.com/. A free online community to inspire women to appreciate and celebrate female friendship, founded in 2006 by Debba Haupert.

Meetup: Women's Friendship Groups. http://womens-friendship-group .meetup.com/. Meetup is a free network to help people self-organize into groups for friendship and community action.

wowOwow: The Women on the Web. http://www.wowowow.com/about/. A free online community created, run, and written by journalists and film and television celebrities, including Lesley Stahl, Liz Smith, Whoopi Goldberg, Candice Bergen, Lily Tomlin, Jane Wagner, Jean Chatzky, Cynthia McFadden, and Marlo Thomas, among others; "conversation" on various topics for women over forty.